How to use *explore*

Issue 116

The 92 daily readings in this issue of *Explore* are designed to help you understand and apply the Bible as you read it each day.

1 Find a time you can read the Bible each day

2 Find a place where you can be quiet and think

3 Ask God to help you understand

4 Carefully read through the Bible passage for today

5 Study the verses with *Explore*, taking time to think

6 Pray about what you have read

It's serious!

We suggest that you allow 15 minutes each day to work through the Bible passage with the notes. It should be a meal, not a snack! Readings from other parts of the Bible can throw valuable light on the study passage. These cross-references can be skipped if you are already feeling full up, but will expand your grasp of the Bible. *Explore* uses the NIV2011 Bible translation, but you can also use it with the NIV1984 or ESV translations.

On most days a prayer section will encourage you to stop and pray through the lessons—but it is always important to allow time to pray for God's Spirit to bring his word to life, and to shape the way we think and live through it.

We're serious!

All of us who work on *Explore* share a passion for getting the Bible into people's lives. We fiercely hold to the Bible as God's word—to honour and follow, not to explain away.

thegoodbook COMPANY

BIBLICAL | RELEVANT | ACCESSIBLE

Welcome to **explore**

Being a Christian isn't a skill you learn, nor is it a lifestyle choice. It's about having a real relationship with the living God through his Son, Jesus Christ. The Bible tells us that this relationship is like a marriage.

It's important to start with this, because it is easy to view the practice of daily Bible reading as a Christian duty, or a hard discipline that is just one more thing to get done in our busy lives.

But the Bible is God speaking to us: opening his mind to us on how he thinks, what he wants for us and what his plans are for the world. And most importantly, it tells us what he has done for us in sending his Son, Jesus Christ, into the world. It's the way that the Spirit shows Jesus to us, and changes us as we behold his glory.

Here are a few suggestions for making your time with God more of a joy than a burden:

- *Time:* Find a time when you will not be disturbed. Many people have found that the morning is the best time as it sets you up for the day. But whatever works for you is right for you.
- *Place:* Jesus says that we are not to make a great show of our religion *(see Matthew 6:5-6)*, but rather, to pray with the door to our room shut. Some people plan to get to work a few minutes earlier and get their Bible out in an office or some other quiet corner.
- *Prayer:* Although *Explore* helps with specific prayer ideas from the passage, do try to develop your own lists to pray through. Use the flap inside the back cover to help with this. And allow what you read in the Scriptures to shape what you pray for yourself, the world and others.
- *Feast:* You can use the "Bible in a year" line at the bottom of each page to help guide you through the entire Scriptures throughout 2026. This year, you will have an Old Testament and a New Testament passage to read, enjoy and reflect on each day. Over the course of the year, you'll read through the entire Bible once.
- *Share:* As the saying goes, *expression deepens impression.* So try to cultivate the habit of sharing with others what you have learned. Why not join our Facebook group to share your encouragements, questions and prayer requests? Search for *Explore: For your daily walk with God.*

And enjoy it! As you read God's word and God's Spirit works in your mind and your heart, you are going to see Jesus, and appreciate more of his love for you and his promises to you. That's amazing!

Carl Laferton is the Co-CEO and Publisher of The Good Book Company

JOHN: The Father's love

Last time we were in John's Gospel, we learned to rejoice in the cross. Today, the apostle gives us two more reasons for joy, whatever our circumstances.

You are loved

Read John 16:23-28

- *How many times is the Father mentioned here?*
- *Why does Jesus say he won't pray for his followers (v 26)?*
- *What new relationship will they have with the Father?*

When Jesus says "in my name", he means: *on the basis of who I am and what I have done for you on the cross.* To ask "in Jesus' name" means to ask on the basis, not of any good in us, but of what Jesus has done for us.

Jesus does not have to ask the Father to love us. The Father has loved us steadily, freely and wonderfully, from all eternity. "The Father himself loves you" (v 27).

Pray

When you lie awake because there are worries on your mind, try this experiment. Before you think about your worries, say to yourself, "I am a Christian because the Father loves me, steadily, freely and for ever". Now go back to your worries. They'll still be there, but you may see them differently.

You are saved

Read John 16:29-32

- *The disciples don't understand fully—but what have they finally seemed to grasp (v 30)?*
- *What tone of voice is verse 31, do you think?*
- *When Jesus dies on the cross, who won't be with him, and who will (v 32)?*
- *What does this tell us about who deserves praise for people being saved?*

That's a relief, actually, because it means the cross is 100% about what he does for us, and 0% about what we can do for him.

Notice that the cross is a rescue done by both Father and Son together, right the way up to that terrible moment when Father and Son are separated: "My God, my God, why have you forsaken me?" (Mark 15:34).

Read John 16:33

- *Why has Jesus told his friends "these things"?*
- *When troubles come (and they will), what will they need to remember?*

Apply

Verse 33 is the last thing recorded by John that Jesus says to all his disciples before the cross.

- *In which areas of your life do you particularly need to remember Jesus' encouragements of verse 33?*

The Father up in lights

Sometimes a theatre puts the name of a famous actor or actress up in lights outside, so everyone will know about them. "Glory" means something like that.

In today's section, Jesus begins a prayer which will take up the rest of the chapter.

Why does Jesus pray?

Why would Jesus pray this prayer out loud so the disciples can hear it? He doesn't need to. The Father would hear a private prayer just as well!

Read John 17:13

- *What reason does Jesus give?*
- *How does Jesus want us to react to what we overhear in this prayer?*

Remember that as we go through it.

The glory of the cross

Read John 17:1

- *What is Jesus praying for?*

TIME OUT

Read John 12:23-33

- *What "hour" has arrived (notice verse 33)?*

Notice the link between being "glorified" and being "lifted up" on the cross.

How amazing that on the cross we see Jesus in lights, and therefore the Father in lights. There we see God more clearly than anywhere else.

The gift of eternal life

Read John 17:2-3

- *What does "eternal life" mean?*

It's a relational thing—living in relationship with the Father and the Son.

- *Who gives eternal life?*
- *Who does he give it to?*

Notice the supremacy of the Father and the wonderful submission of Jesus.

Pray

Thank the Father that he gave you to Jesus, and thank Jesus that by his death he gave you an eternal relationship with himself and the Father.

The finished work

Read John 17:4-5

Jesus "finishes" the work he came to do at the cross. The same word is used in John 19:30. In his prayer Jesus anticipates that terrible and wonderful completion of the work of giving eternal life.

- *How do you think the cross brings the Father glory?*

Jesus' rescue mission was given him by the Father. When he completes it, we see not only Jesus but also the Father's love. The cross was the Father's idea first!

The Father revealed

Why would you say that the Bible matters? Today we're going to learn one wonderful reason.

The "eternity" gift

Read John 17:6

- *Who does Jesus reveal the Father to?*
- *Does anything strike you about how Jesus describes these people?*

If someone asks you when God rescued you, the first answer is that the Father rescued you in eternity past when he gave you to Jesus, long before you were born!

The words of eternal life

Read John 17:7-8

- *What have Christian disciples obeyed and come to know (v 6-8)?*

This is a single message (a "word") given to us in a book ("words"). It's not just the words Jesus literally spoke on earth; it's the whole message about Jesus in the Bible, including what his apostles wrote about him in the New Testament and what the prophets had written about him in the Old Testament.

Notice that it is by the message and words of the Bible that we grasp who Jesus really is.

Apply

- *Why is it so important to go to a church where people really trust, obey and teach the Bible?*

Belonging to Father and Son

Read John 17:9

What does Jesus mean by saying "for they are yours"? Surely they were the Father's, but now the Father has given them to Jesus!

Read John 17:10

All the people who really belong to Jesus really belong to the Father! The Father and Jesus are so closely united that they have everything and everyone in common. So if we belong to Jesus, we belong to the Father, and if we belong to the Father, we belong to Jesus.

Pray

Spend a moment thinking about belonging to the Father and belonging to Jesus, and praise the Father and the Son for this amazing privilege.

The wounds of love

Spend a couple of minutes thinking through all the things in your life that you can thank God for. Did you mention suffering…?

The stunning conclusion to this section of Psalm 119 in verses 65-72 says that suffering is used by God *for our good*—it helps us to learn to love him and obey his word. The psalmist is not saying that suffering is good; it is not. If it were, there would be suffering in the new creation. Suffering is like a knife: it can be wielded by a mugger to harm us, or by a surgeon to heal us. God is a wise, kind surgeon, and this section teaches us that suffering is his scalpel.

Surrounded but firm

Read Psalm 119:49-56

- *What circumstances does the psalmist face in these verses?*
- *What is his comfort (v 50, 52)?*

Committed, whatever

Read Psalm 119:56-64

There is something wonderfully simple about the psalmist's response when God speaks, according to these first two sections.

- *What does he do (v 56, 60)?*
- *What else does he resolve to do?*

TIME OUT

The first two sections use a variety of terms for God's word. Some are clear to us: "words", "ways", "promises", "commands"—others less so. "Laws" translates two words. One is a general word for all that God teaches; the other refers to his judgments about what is right and what is wrong. "Statutes" are words that bear witness to who God is. "Precepts" are the detailed application of God's word to the circumstances of life. "Decrees" emphasises the permanent, binding nature of what God says.

School of hard knocks

Read Psalm 119:65-72

- *What does the psalmist declare about God at the heart of this section (v 68)?*
- *Does he say this because his life is easy?*
- *What impact have the hardships he has faced had upon him (v 67, 71)?*

Apply

Do we realise that to pray, "God make me more like Christ; help me walk in your ways", may well be to pray for suffering?

- *When have you seen difficulties in life lead to spiritual growth—either in your own life or the lives of others?*

Pray

Pray that you would share the psalmist's conviction in verse 68 that God is good. Pray too that when suffering comes—which it surely will—it would drive you to God in dependence, rather than away from him in bitterness.

The Father's protection

It can be pretty scary to be a Christian in many parts of the world. Even in so-called "Christian" countries it's not easy to live publicly as a real Christian. How safe are we?

Alone in a hostile world

Read John 17:11a

- *What is going to happen to Jesus?*
- *What about the eleven apostles?*
- *Why do you think they might be scared?*

TIME OUT

Read John 15:18-24; 16:1-4

This hatred from the world is what they, and we, ought to expect. No wonder they are scared!

Protection by union

Read John 17:11b-12

- *What does Jesus pray for his disciples?*
- *How is the Father going to protect them?*

The "name" that the Father gave Jesus is who Jesus is: God the eternal Son in intimate fellowship with the Father. Jesus protected them by bringing them into fellowship with the Father and the Son. Any attack on them was an attack on God!

Jesus and the Father are "one" (10:30). Christians are "one". Rather than teaching that we must work hard to get along, here Jesus is saying that God has brought us into fellowship with the Father and the Son.

Pray

Spend some time now praising the Father and the Son for bringing you into fellowship with them and with all other real Christians. Thank God for guaranteeing your eternal safety.

Hated but rejoicing

Read John 17:13-15

- *Why does Jesus pray this prayer out loud so they can overhear it (v 13)?*
- *What is going to happen to us in the world (v 14)?*
- *Can we expect to be taken out of situations where this happens (v 15)?*

Apply

We need consciously to remind ourselves of the wonderful protection from the Father for which Jesus prayed. When it's tough being a Christian, never forget this.

- *In what circumstances in your life do you particularly need to remember this?*
- *How will it make a difference to your emotions? To your actions?*

Bible in a year: Ezekiel 37 – 39 • John 18:1-18

Set apart for a mission

When explorers get ready to be sent somewhere dangerous, they need to separate themselves from the comfortable life they will leave behind.

They may need to train physically, and to keep certain disciplines. It's like that for Jesus' church.

Read John 17:16-19

Set apart for mission

Jesus often said the Father had "sent" him on a rescue mission. Now he sends his followers "into the world".

This doesn't mean that our mission is identical to his. It just means that we too are "sent" people. His mission was to die to rescue the world; our mission is to take his rescue message into the world.

Set apart by the Bible

- *What relationship does the Christian have with the world in which they live (v 16, 18)?*
- *What does this look like in practice, do you think?*

Set apart

- *In verse 17, what does Jesus pray?*
- *How is the Father going to "sanctify" us (set us apart for a task)?*

Here, "word" is not referring to Jesus (as in John 1:1) but to the message of the Bible. Tenacious loyalty to the Bible will set us apart from the world (and from any part of the church which is worldly) to be missionaries for Jesus.

Apply

- *Can you think of examples of how your values as a Christian are different from the values of non-Christians?*
- *How does our culture disagree with the message of the Bible?*
- *What should we do when tempted to compromise on these issues, or when church ministers begin to fudge them?*

Set apart by the cross

- *What does Jesus say he does for himself?*

To "sanctify" means here to set himself apart for his death on the cross. Like a holy sacrifice in Old Testament times, Jesus has to go alone to the cross, set apart from the world.

- *Why does Jesus say he is doing this?*

Only Jesus' death for us on the cross can set us apart, making us fit for mission.

Pray

Pray that your life as a Christian will always go back to the cross as your starting point, and always be shaped by the cross when called upon to make tough decisions for Jesus.

What *Jesus* prays for *us*

How do you feel when someone says they are praying for you? I guess it depends on what they are praying, and whether you think God will answer them!

Today we listen in to a prayer for us that God will most certainly answer, because of the one who prays it. So let's rejoice in what he prays.

Prayed for by Jesus

Read John 17:20

- *Who is Jesus now praying for?*
- *Why is this amazing for us today?*

Notice that these people don't just believe in some vague notion of "Jesus". They believe in the real, historical Jesus through the message of the apostles, which is the Bible. Jesus is not praying here for anyone who might call themselves a Christian; he is praying for people who believe the Bible message about the real Jesus.

Unity in the gospel

Read John 17:21-23

- *From these verses, what is Christian unity?*

Christians are brought into fellowship with the Father and the Son, and reflect their unity. So they don't need to try to create an outward institutional religious unity; they are given an inner spiritual unity.

In fact, outward unity is of no value, and can be dangerous, if there is no underlying unity brought by a shared fellowship in Christ and commitment to the gospel.

TIME OUT

Have you known Jesus-centred, Bible-based unity with unlikely people, perhaps in different cultures? Rejoice if you have!

Prospect of glory

Read John 17:24

- *What does Jesus ask here?*
- *Why is it so brilliant to hear Jesus praying this for you and me?*

It will be wonderful to see Jesus as he is, and to see the love the Father has for him in all its fullness.

Wonder of gospel love

Read John 17:25-26

Jesus "will continue to make" the Father known. He does this by the Holy Spirit today. Look at the end of verse 26. What happens when men and women come to know the Father? The love within the Trinity overflows to us!

Pray

This love is the only force that can remake a broken world. Pray that it will be seen in your local church.

What do you get most excited about? Compare this with seeing the Son in glory, and pray that your heart will be thrilled by that glorious prospect.

Bible in a year: Ezekiel 42 – 44 • John 19:1-22

Who's in control?

It isn't always obvious who is in control. When Jesus is arrested, John prompts us to ask, who is really in control...

... when Jesus is arrested?

Read John 18:1-3

- *Who seems to be in control?*

But think: why does Jesus choose to go to this particular spot when he knows that Judas knows the place? Jesus is not trying to escape. He is arrested because he knows it is the right time to be arrested.

... when Jesus is identified?

Read John 18:4-7

- *What does Jesus already know?*
- *What name do the soldiers have on their arrest warrant?*

It is a purely human name from a very ordinary place.

- *How does Jesus answer, three times?*

Literally, he is saying simply, "I am".

- *What effect does this unexpected "name" have on them (v 6)?*

"I am" is God's name for himself. The soldiers thought they were arresting an ordinary human troublemaker; but here they're confronted with the name and power of God himself.

... when Jesus protects his own?

Read John 18:8-9

- *Why was Jesus concerned to ensure none of the disciples were arrested with him?*

... when Jesus drinks the cup?

Read John 18:10-11

TIME OUT

Read Psalm 75:8; Revelation 16:19

These are just two examples of what the "cup" means in Bible language.

- *What does it mean for the innocent Jesus to "drink the cup the Father has given me" (John 18:11)?*

Simon Peter has already volunteered to give his life for Jesus (13:37)—in battle, fighting his enemies. What he now needs to understand is that Jesus will give his life for Simon—on the cross, bearing his punishment.

Apply

- *Why does it matter greatly that we remember God is in full control as we consider the cross of Christ?*

The cost of being an insider

We want to be insiders, and hate feeling as if we're outsiders. Whoever the "in crowd" may be, we naturally want to belong with them. But there is often a cost...

Powerful opposition

Read John 18:12-14

- *Who is against Jesus?*

The most powerful people in the land are related to each other, and all are determined to kill Jesus. Annas and his relatives held power for 34 years out of 36 between AD 6 and AD 41. Annas was a nasty, corrupt political fixer.

Apply

- *Who are the most powerful people in your neighbourhood, workplace or society? Are they pro-Jesus or not?*

Outsiders and insiders

Read John 18:15-16

Look carefully at the language of being outside and being inside.

- *What is the inside place (v 15)?*
- *Where does Peter end up (v 16)?*

This is the place of all human power. Peter's move from outside to inside is a picture of what we all long to do, to get "in" with the powerful people.

Apply

- *Which group of people would you naturally most like to be "in" with, in your workplace, neighbourhood, college or school?*

The cost of going in

Read John 18:17

- *What question does Peter have to answer in order to be allowed in?*
- *How does he answer?*

It is so easy, so natural, so understandable, and so terribly wrong. Notice how Jesus is described only as "this man"; who would want to be associated with him, now that he is under arrest?

Standing in the cold

Read John 18:18

It's a sad picture. These people are in the dark and cold (literally and spiritually) and have to light and warm themselves with a fire. And now Peter is "standing" with them, "warming himself" in the in-crowd.

Pray

Think ahead to when someone next challenges you about being a Christian.

- *What will you be tempted to say? Why?*

Pray that you will give courageous testimony to Jesus, especially when people around you despise him.

Hated without reason

We can't blame people for treating us badly when we've treated them badly. But Jesus was hated with no valid reason at all.

Open teaching

Read John 18:19-20

The "high priest" in verse 19 is still Annas. Even when people had retired from being high priest they kept the title.

- *What exactly does Annas ask about in verse 19?*

He wants to know what kind of a political movement this is—and it's a threatening question for people like Peter.

- *How does Jesus answer (v 20)?*

Of course, Jesus did instruct his disciples privately (such as in chapters 13 – 16). But what he said privately was the same message as the one he gave publicly. He had no secret agenda, and nothing to hide.

TIME OUT

Read 2 Corinthians 4:2

Think about how our openness about the gospel ought to follow the brave openness of Jesus. There ought to be no part of the Bible's teaching that we keep secret, or only talk about when we're with people who are already Christians.

Open testimony

Read John 18:21

- *Who will be able to report what Jesus has taught?*

Notice that this is exactly what Peter has not done (v 15-18) and will not do (v 25-27) in his denials.

Apply

We cannot give eye-witness testimony to Jesus. Only the apostles could do that. But we can speak up accurately and bravely to tell people what the apostles have told us Jesus said, found in the New Testament. We ought to do that.

Unfair condemnation

Read John 18:22-24

- *Why is the official angry?*
- *How does Jesus defend himself?*

Notice the word "testify". He is inviting them to give eye-witness testimony to prove he is wrong, but they can't. This shows the trial is completely unfair.

Pray

Thank the Lord Jesus for suffering this unreasonable hatred on his way to the cross, for our sake.

A light for dark paths

Where does your mind go when it is in neutral? What ideas do you think about? What thoughts about yourself, or others, or God, do you have on loop play in your mind?

At this time of year, we can already hear Christmas music in some shops—an endless loop of cheesy classics. This section, which marks the halfway point in Psalm 119, encourages us to make sure that the background music in our minds is healthy. This is more important than ever when life is hard, as it is throughout these verses.

Trusting my Creator

Read Psalm 119:73-80

- *What is life like for the psalmist at the moment (v 75, 78)?*
- *What reasons are there in these verses for trusting in God?*

How wonderful to know that the one who gives us commands knows us better than we know ourselves—even better than a parent knows their own child. That's because he is our Creator.

- *What impact does the psalmist's trust during hard times have on other believers?*

Clinging to my Saviour

Read Psalm 119:81-88

Spurgeon described this as the "midnight" of the psalm. Seven of these verses describe struggle, opposition and suffering. Work through them, looking to see how the psalmist responds each time.

Relying on my Lord

Read Psalm 119:89-96

- *Why, according to these verses does the psalmist trust in God's word?*

I used to be a lawyer. I spent long hours studying the rules of civil litigation—only to find that the rulebook was going to be replaced. Everything I'd learned was useless. But God does not change. So we can trust that the promises he made yesterday hold true today, and will still hold true tomorrow. His commands are "boundless" (v 96).

TIME OUT

We might admire the psalmist's resolute trust that God will save him, but remarkably, we can be *even more* confident. We have seen Jesus Christ more oppressed than anyone—persecuted to death. But we have also seen him rescued from the grave by God to victorious eternal life. We have seen God deliver on his promises to rescue his Son. As we look to Jesus, we see proof that we can trust this God to save and keep us too.

Pray

Pray that we would grow in trust and confidence that God's promises can be relied on.

Use verses 81-88 to pray too for the millions of Christians around the world who know the oppression spoken of in these verses as their literal, daily experience.

Bible in a year: Song of Songs 4 – 5 • Ephesians 1

The dangers of discipleship

Have you ever listened to a politician being asked a question they don't want to answer? There is something pathetic about dishonesty and cover-ups.

Where Peter stands

Read John 18:25

- *Look back at verse 18. Where is Peter "standing" and who is he with?*

In verse 25 he is still "standing" there. Where he "stands" physically is a picture of where he belongs spiritually.

- *Why do you think it is a dangerous place to stand?*

Apply

Think about a place where you go regularly, perhaps a workplace, or club, or school.

- *What would it look like to be there physically without belonging there spiritually?*

What Peter is asked

In verse 21 Jesus invited people to ask "those who heard me" to give testimony about him. Now this is exactly what happens, as they ask Peter.

- *What is the difference between the question of verse 25 and the question he had been asked before in verse 17?*

It's the same question. But as the passage makes clear, this time it's asked not just by one unimportant person (a servant girl) but by "they".

- *Look back at verse 18. Who are they?*
- *Why do you think this second question was more frightening than the first?*

Read John 18:26

- *Why do you think this third question is the most frightening of all (verse 10 may help)?*

Apply

- *Why is it uncomfortable to be asked questions about Jesus and your faith in him? What is it that makes you feel frightened?*

Failure is no surprise

Read John 18:27

- *What is the significance of the cock crowing? (Look back at 13:38.)*

Jesus was not taken by surprise. He knew none of the disciples were ready to give testimony to him yet. One day they would, but not until the Holy Spirit was given to enable them to.

Pray

Thank Jesus that he knows we can't stand up for him on our own.

Pray for the Holy Spirit to help you to say clearly that you belong to him next time you are asked.

Hypocrisy and hatred

Is there anything about Jesus you find difficult to like? Think back to when you weren't a real Christian, if you can. What was it about Jesus that, to be honest, you just didn't like?

Outside and inside

Read John 18:28

- *Why did the Jewish leaders stay outside the Roman governor's palace (the Praetorium)?*

It's an irony that they minded so much about a bit of ritual defilement (going into a Gentile's house) while not caring about judicial murder.

TIME OUT

The whole passage from John 18:28 – 19:16 alternates between "outside" and "inside" the Praetorium. Look through the passage to see the seven different scenes, which move between inside and outside.

The blank charge sheet

Read John 18:29-30

- *What question does Pilate ask?*
- *How do they answer?*

They avoid the question! They've got nothing concrete to bring to Pilate to get a conviction, so they just suggest to Pilate that he can trust them, that they wouldn't waste his time with some trumped-up charge. Ironically, of course, that's exactly what they are doing!

Notice the words "hand over". This is an important theme. Those who think they are the people of God hand their rightful King over to the Gentile ruler. So they prove they aren't really the people of God at all.

Which law?

Read John 18:31

There is a play on the word "law" (the second time, the NIV translates it "right").

Jesus is not going to be condemned under God's law (Jewish law) but under Gentile law. This reinforces his innocence; God's law has nothing against him.

Crucified

Read John 18:32

- *Why did the Jewish leaders hand Jesus over to Pilate?*

TIME OUT

Read John 3:14; 12:32-34

- *Why was it specifically necessary for Jesus to die by being crucified ?*

Notice the Old Testament picture of the bronze snake (Numbers 21:8-9). "Lifted up" has the double meaning of "lifted up in glory" and "lifted up on a cross".

Pray

Think about hypocrisy. How easy it is to pretend to keep religious laws while our hearts are wrong towards God! Pray for a pure heart.

Bible in a year: 1 Samuel 1 – 3 • Ephesians 3

The King and the terrorist

Sometimes evil is disguised, and sometimes evil is brought right out into the open and seen for what it is. We see an example of each in today's passage.

The King of the Jews

Read John 18:33-34

- *What does Pilate want to know?*
- *Why do you think he asks this question?*

It's simple politics. He wants to know whether Jesus is a terrorist or rebel.

- *Why do you think Jesus fires this question back?*

He wants to know whether it's a Roman question ("your own idea"), in which case the answer is "no"; or a Jewish question ("others"), in which case the answer may be "yes". It depends what sort of king.

Read John 18:35-36

Pilate can't understand what Jesus is getting at.

- *How does Jesus answer in verse 36 and what reason does he give to support his answer?*

Look back to verses 10-11 to see an illustration of this.

Witness to the truth

Read John 18:37-38

How does Jesus define what him being King means?

- *Who has Jesus been bearing witness to, all through his life?*

He is the true witness, who perfectly shows men and women the Father God. He is God's Ruler for the world.

- *Who listens to what Jesus says about the Father?*

Is Pilate one of them? It doesn't look like it, sadly.

Apply

The test of real Christianity is believing that Jesus perfectly reveals the Father, and so submitting to all that Jesus teaches in the Bible.

Murderous hearts

Read John 18:38-40

How deeply they hate Jesus, that they prefer to have a violent robber, a kind of terrorist, released instead of him. Notice the contrast between what Pilate says about Jesus (v 38b) and what John tells us about Barabbas (v 40). The world prefers guilt and violence to peace and innocence.

The irony is that the innocent man suffers on behalf of the guilty. Barabbas can only be set free because the innocent Jesus suffers in his place.

Pray

Thank God that innocent Jesus suffered to set you, guilty of sin as you are, free.

Bible in a year: 1 Samuel 4 – 6 • Ephesians 4

Here is the man!

One of the surprising things about Jesus' sufferings was that the ringleaders were the most religious men of his day. But it is the same today.

There are no enemies more deeply hostile to real Christianity than church people who don't know the real Christ.

Mocked and flogged

Read John 19:1-3

Roman flogging was brutal, inflicted by a whip with thongs loaded with pieces of bone or metal. It ripped open flesh and sometimes killed its victims.

The mock "crown" had long spikes from the date palm, up to 30cm long, adding to the bleeding and pain of Jesus. The purple robe and the crown mock him as a pathetic wannabe king. It is a picture of painful and utterly undeserved disgrace.

Pray

An old hymn puts it well: "In my place condemned he stood, sealed my pardon with his blood. Hallelujah! What a Saviour!"

Spend time thanking your Saviour now.

Here is the man

Read John 19:4-6

Pilate has Jesus mocked and scourged to try to appease the Jewish leaders. But all the time he knows Jesus is innocent. He says so twice more.

"Here is (or "behold") the man!" (v 5) is ambiguous. Pilate no doubt meant by it: *Look at this pathetic human being. This isn't a king!* But surely John expects us to remember that the "man" we are invited to look at is not just a man; he is the eternal Son of God.

Jesus had to be fully human to bear our sin; but he also had to be more than just human. He had to be divine as well, so that he could live a completely innocent human life.

The Son of God

Read John 19:7

Pilate has found Jesus innocent of any political crime.

- *What religious crime do the Jewish leaders accuse Jesus of committing?*
- *What possibility about Jesus are they resolutely refusing to consider?*

These men's religion and self-made laws (v 7) have brought them status, influence and respect. This allows them to feel self-righteous. And since Jesus would overturn all of this, they would rather kill God's Son than give it up.

Apply

- *Are there any areas of your life where you find it easy to love "religion" instead of Jesus?*
- *How is it possible for us to act in our lives as Pilate does here?*

Bible in a year: 1 Samuel 7 – 9 • Ephesians 5:1-16

No king but Caesar?

They say that "he who pays the piper calls the tune". There will be some people on earth who have influence over us; we naturally want to do what they say.

Where are you from?

Read John 19:8-9

- *Why is Pilate frightened?*

Look back to verse 7. He is a superstitious man with a bad conscience, and so is easily unsettled.

- *What does he ask Jesus in verse 9?*

It's a question that has been discussed before in John's Gospel (7:27-29; 8:14).

- *Why do you think Jesus doesn't answer him?*

There's an echo here of Isaiah 53:7: "He did not open his mouth ... as a sheep before its shearers is silent, so he did not open his mouth".

Guilty or more guilty?

Read John 19:10-11

- *Why is Pilate surprised at Jesus' silence?*
- *How does Jesus reply?*

TIME OUT

Read Romans 13:1-7

Notice that Paul teaches the same as Jesus about human authority.

- *What does Jesus conclude at the end of John 19:11?*
- *Who handed Jesus over to Pilate?*
- *Why are the Jewish leaders even more guilty than Pilate?*

Somehow the depth of their malice is greater. Pilate is a weak leader trying rather badly and inconsistently to do his job. The Jewish leaders actively hate Jesus and have set out to destroy him. They are certainly not doing their job of shepherding God's people!

No king but Caesar

Read John 19:12-16a

"Caesar" means the Roman emperor (Tiberius at that time). To be "Caesar's friend" was an almost-official, privileged status. Pilate is terrified of losing it, so he loses his own soul instead. In fact, he was disgraced by the emperor a few years later anyway. Pilate mocks the Jewish leaders. But they hate Jesus so much they put up with the mockery, to get him crucified.

There's great irony here as the priests say, "We have no king but Caesar"! It is a strange thing to hear Jews say. Yet at a very deep level it is true; they are serving the powers of this world and not the one true God. Everyone does one or the other.

Pray

Pray that you may be able to say, and mean, the opposite of the priests: "I have no king but Jesus".

The cross a throne

Most kings rule from a throne. We expect presidents and prime ministers to have the trappings of state and glory. And yet Jesus rules the world from a cross.

The place

Read John 19:16b-17

Picture the scene, as Jesus carries the crossbeam until he is exhausted, and Simon of Cyrene has to be conscripted to carry it the rest of the way (Luke 23:26). He is taken to "the place of the Skull", which may be a place that looks like a skull or just a burial place. It is a place of death, uncleanness and separation from God.

The company

Read John 19:18

- *What kind of company is Jesus now keeping?*

On the cross, he is identified with sinners and carries on his own shoulders the sin of the world.

You and I ought to have been on those crosses next to Jesus. We deserve that terrible death for our rebellion against the God who made us. But Jesus took our place and died our death.

Pray

Spend some time looking at the scene in your mind's eye: and then spend some time thanking your King that he hung on a cross in your place.

The inscription

Read John 19:19-20

- *What does the inscription say?*

Notice how it combines Jesus' human identification (his name and town) with his rightful title.

- *How does John emphasise the significance of this inscription above the cross (v 20)?*

The inscription is written in three languages. Pontius Pilate preaches the gospel to the world! In the end, Jesus is recognised as the King as he hangs on the cross.

Read John 19:21-22

- *What is the priests' problem?*
- *How does Pilate respond?*

Apply

Pilate acted more truly than he realised. He thought he was mocking and irritating the Jewish leaders. In fact he was proclaiming the gospel.

Jesus really is the King, not only of the Jews, but of all the world.

We ought to come to his cross and bow before him in obedient worship.

Words that work

Did you know that the Bible is the world's most shop-lifted book? Yes—not only is it the best-selling book in the world every year, but it is also the one most often stolen!

Today's three sections of Psalm 119 give two big reasons why people will do anything to get their hands on this wonderful book!

The Maker's instructions

Read Psalm 119:97-104

We're almost 100 verses into this psalm, and most of those verses express love for God's word. This section is no different.

- *But what is the reason for loving God's word that we find in verses 97-100?*
- *What image does the writer use in verse 103? Has this been your experience?*
- *What does this understanding lead the writer to do in verse 104?*
- *In what times or situations have you found that obeying God's word is the best way to live in this life?*

A light to lead us home

Read Psalm 119:105-120

Verse 105 is a "tea-towel verse"—that is, it's known and loved by many but is often wrenched out of context. The rest of the stanza helps us work out what it means...

- *Look at verses 106, 109 and 112. Is the writer concerned with guidance when life is unclear or with obedience?*

What makes things harder is that the writer is surrounded by enemies (v 109-110).

- *In spite of that, what resolution does he make?*
- *Have you ever been intimidated by others into disobeying God?*

Often my prayers focus on asking God for guidance in tricky decisions. That is important, but we would be wise to spend just as much time asking God for courage to obey him when the right path is clearly lit but we know going that way will be costly.

- *The focus shifts in verses 117-119. What is the most important reason to cling to God's word?*
- *What will happen at the end of time?*

God's word is not only the best way to live in this life; it is the only way to find salvation for eternal life as we learn about Jesus Christ (2 Timothy 3:15).

Apply

- *Are there areas in your life where you are finding it hard to trust that God's ways are best?*
- *What would obedience look like in those areas? What would it take for you to obey joyfully?*

Pray

Pray that God would help you to understand his ways and to see that he knows best. Pray too for courage to obey God when doing what is right will be unpopular or costly.

Bible in a year: 1 Samuel 15 – 16 • 2 Peter 1

Cast out of this world

Death is a terrible thing—and it is something that, whether we try to ignore it or not, we will all experience. The reality of death ought to horrify us—if it were not for Jesus.

No protection

Read John 19:23-24

- *What happens at the foot of the cross?*
- *Why is this particularly significant (v 24)?*

TIME OUT

In verse 24, John is quoting from Psalm 22.

Read Psalm 22:12-19: see and feel the terror of David in the psalm, and think about how these sufferings were fulfilled by Jesus.

It's worth dwelling on the truth that Jesus was stripped absolutely naked. Don't believe the pious paintings which show him with a loincloth. He died with literally nothing to call his own. The alternative to Jesus being naked for us is that one day, at God's final judgment, we will be stripped naked so that every word, thought, and deed will be exposed for the universe to see, and then we will be left with nothing.

Pray

Think about the shame and disgrace that Jesus endured, and thank him for doing that for *you*.

No mother

Read John 19:25

Two women are unnamed. Jesus' mother, Mary, is never named in John's Gospel. By looking at the parallel passages in the other Gospels, it seems the second woman may have been Salome, the mother of John and his brother James. The other two are "Mary, the wife of Clopas" and "Mary Magdalene", who (as we'll see) becomes the first witness of the resurrection.

These courageous women were the last at the cross.

Read John 19:26-27

- *What is staggering about what Jesus is doing in these verses?*

The "disciple whom Jesus loved" is almost certainly John, the Gospel-writer. He writes as an eye-witness and can never forget this little scene of love.

Jesus is separated from his nearest and dearest in this life. However much others may grieve for him, he dies alone.

Pray

Ask God to help you look after your parents, if they are alive. But more importantly, thank Jesus for being willing to be separated from all human comfort, simply to save us.

Mission accomplished!

The job Jesus was given by the Father was more difficult, more painful and more terrible than any mission any human being has been given, before or since.

The thirst

Read John 19:28-29

Now read Psalm 69:21. This is probably the Scripture Jesus was fulfilling. It describes the terrible sufferings of an innocent man. There are few human sufferings more acute than thirst.

TIME OUT

Read John 4:13-14; 7:37-39

- *What was Jesus offering on both these occasions?*
- *What was Jesus sorely lacking as he died?*

As we look at the cross, we understand that Jesus can only give "living water" to others because he himself suffered this terrible thirst on the cross. Our life is at the cost of his death, our living water at the cost of his thirst.

The completion

Read John 19:30

Jesus had said (in 4:34) that the only thing that mattered to him was to finish the mission the Father had given him—to glorify his Father by saving his people.

- *What is so wonderful about Jesus' last words?*
- *What does it teach us about the cross?*

We cannot add anything to the finished work of Christ on the cross. He has done everything that is necessary for our sins to be forgiven and for us to become sons and daughters of God. To try to add something (by being religious, going to church, reading our Bibles, living moral lives...) is like trying to improve a Monet painting by adding some brushstrokes of our own. However much care we take, we won't be able to add to the masterpiece: we'll deface and destroy it.

Apply

Check that in your own heart you are not thinking you can help Jesus save you.

The final breath

At the end of verse 30 Jesus "gave up his spirit". The Son of God stopped breathing and died. But his last words also remind us of his control over events, even with his hands pinned to a wooden plank. He suffered in our place, experiencing hell until the full measure of our sin had been paid for and "it [was] finished". And then, his mission complete, he ceased to breathe. And even that was his choice. What a Saviour!

Life by his death

John loves telling us eye-witness truth in a way that points to a deeper truth. Today's passage points us to a wonderful truth.

Not a bone broken

Read John 19:31-37

- *What was the problem facing the Jewish authorities?*
- *How did they solve it?*

Often crucifixion victims took several days to die. But if they had their legs broken, they could no longer push their bodies up to breathe, and so they died immediately.

- *What did they discover when they came to Jesus (v 33)?*

Read John 19:36

This is a reference to the Passover lamb (see, for example, Exodus 12:46). John is pointing us back 1,500 years, to when God's people put a lamb's blood on their doors in Egypt so that God's judgment would "pass over" their houses.

So, the physical fact of Jesus' legs not being broken points to the deeper truth that Jesus is the ultimate Passover lamb, who died in our place.

Blood and water

Read John 19:34

- *What do you think this meant?*

Read John 19:35-37

- *Why do you think it was so important that John actually saw this and is a trustworthy witness of the blood and water?*

This testimony is necessary for our faith. How? It's puzzling, isn't it? The main thing is that we can be sure Jesus was really human and really died. If you have time, explore the other clues below.

TIME OUT

The first clue is in verse 37. This is a quotation from **Zechariah 12:10**, where God himself is "pierced", and the people who pierced him grieve when they realise what they have done. So the piercing of Jesus fulfils this prophecy.

The second clue is in 1 **John 5:6-10**, where water seems to stand for life (as in **John 4:13-14; 7:37-38**), and blood seems to stand for our sin being forgiven by Jesus' death (as in 1 **John 1:7**).

Pray

Thank Jesus that he was really human, really died, and that by his death our sins are really forgiven so that we can receive real new life.

Brave at last

The more successful we are, the more we stand to lose by being Christians. Some people are so successful that they don't dare follow Christ—until they understand the cross.

Joseph of Arimathea

Read John 19:38

- *Until now, what had Joseph believed, and why hadn't he spoken out?*

Back in John 12:42 we learned the extraordinary fact that large numbers of the ruling Jews (the Sanhedrin, etc.) knew that Jesus was genuine but didn't dare say so because they were frightened of the Pharisees (the religious storm-troopers of the day), who might exclude them from respectable religious society. Joseph had been one of them.

Imagine how hard it must have been to ask the Roman governor for the body of a man executed for setting himself up as a rival king to Caesar, and to do so in front of the Jewish religious leaders who had wanted Jesus dead. But at last Joseph comes into the open as a disciple of Jesus.

Nicodemus

Read John 19:39

- *What does John remind us about Nicodemus?*

Read John 3:1-2; 7:45-52

- *Can you see any progress in Nicodemus between chapter 3 and chapter 7?*
- *What response does Nicodemus' rather cautious support for Jesus in chapter 7 get from the other leaders?*
- *How does Nicodemus demonstrate in John 19:39 that he is now firmly and openly on Jesus' side?*

The amount of spices he brings is huge, fit for the burial of a king.

Think how moving it must have been to see these once-powerful men openly professing faith in Jesus at this terrible time when Jesus is dead and there seems to be no hope. There is nothing in it for them; they do this simply out of loyalty and love.

Read John 19:40-42

The simple fact of Jesus' burial is recorded, so we can be quite sure he was really dead and really buried.

Apply

Think how hard it is for you to be an open Christian, perhaps at work.

- *How do these two examples inspire you to stand openly for Jesus when it's really difficult and there is nothing in it for you?*
- *Is there a specific situation in which you need to copy these men, and live openly as a follower of Jesus?*

The inevitable resurrection

"Of course Jesus will rise. What else would you expect?" If someone had said that to you on the evening of Good Friday, I guess you would have been very surprised.

"No," you might have said, "Of course he won't. Dead people stay dead."

The open tomb

Read John 20:1-2

- *What does Mary Magdalene see?*
- *What conclusion does she draw?*

We know from the other Gospels that other women went too, but John focuses on Mary Magdalene, because of what will happen in tomorrow's reading. Mary had seen Jesus buried in a tomb, with a big stone rolled across the entrance (Mark 15:47). She sees the stone gone and assumes grave-robbers have stolen Jesus' body.

The two witnesses

Read John 20:3-7

- *What do the two disciples do that Mary had not done?*
- *What do they see?*

The "other disciple" is almost certainly John himself. They had to bend over because the entrance was probably less than a metre tall. They saw no body—but the burial clothes were still there, all neatly laid out. No grave-robbers would have left the grave-clothes behind, and they certainly wouldn't have tidied everything up!

Believing without understanding

Read John 20:8-9

- *What is different about this second disciple (apart from running faster!)?*

Notice that in verse 6 Peter "saw", but in verse 8 John "saw and believed". That is, he believed the empty tomb meant that Jesus had been raised. That was a wonderful step for John.

But the surprise comes in verse 9.

- *What did John and Peter not yet grasp?*

John believed because of the evidence of his eyes—but not because the Old Testament told them Jesus was bound to be raised.

TIME OUT

Read Psalm 16:8-11; Acts 2:24-32

Since death is the penalty for sin, when a sinless man dies, then if God is fair (which he is), this man is bound to be raised from death. It is inevitable.

Pray

Praise the Father God for being righteous and fair in raising the sinless Jesus from death. Thank him for the eyewitness accounts and Old Testament promises in his word.

Bible in a year: 1 Samuel 27 – 29 • 1 Timothy 3

First to see Jesus

Those who know they owe Christ most will enjoy Christ best. That was true for Mary Magdalene then, and it is true for us today.

Mary of Magdala

Read John 20:10-13

- *Why did Mary stay behind after Peter and John went home?*
- *How does John describe her (v 11)?*

Mary loved Jesus a lot, not with a sexual love, but with a love of gratitude. **Read Luke 8:1-3** and see how she is described. Whatever "seven demons" means, it must have been terrible. Jesus rescued her from deep distress, and she never forgot. Incidentally, "Magdalene" is not her surname, but a reference to the fishing town in Galilee from which she came.

The risen Lord

Read John 20:14-16

Mary was among the last to remain at the cross, and she is first at the tomb. She is the first human being to hear the risen Jesus. Notice that Jesus is known not by sight but by his voice, like the "good shepherd" of John 10:4. It is his words that make him known.

Apply

- *How is this great news for us, living as we do 2,000 years after Jesus returned to heaven?*

A new relationship

Read John 20:17-18

- *Holding on to Jesus is a very natural thing for Mary to do—why does Jesus tell her not to?*

Jesus is in an "in-between" state, risen but not yet ascended. After he has ascended, the Holy Spirit will be sent to make Jesus real in our experience. So Mary can't know Jesus anymore in the old way of a physical friend. But soon she will know him in the new, deeper way of the Holy Spirit.

- *What new relationships does Jesus imply in verse 17?*
- *Why is this seriously exciting?!*

Pray

Thank God that because of Jesus' death you can call him "Father", because the Father of Jesus is now your Father.

Pray that, like Mary, you will realise more of how much you owe to Jesus, and so love him more.

Love that leads to hate

We often think of love and hate as opposites. But when you think about it, love often can—and should—lead to hate.

If I love a relative, I will hate the cancer that ravages them. If I love my city, I will hate the terrorism that brings fear to it. And if I love God and his law, and the honour of his name, then inevitably I will be distressed when he is dishonoured and I will hate evil.

The devoted servant

Read Psalm 119:121-128

- *What things does the writer love or long for in this section?*
- *What things cause them distress?*

Zeal for righteousness

Read Psalm 119:129-144

After the declarations of devotion in the previous section, we get explanations in the next two sections.

- *What reasons are given for why we can love God's word? (See particularly verses 129-130, 137-138, 140, 142-144.)*
- *How does the writer feel about God's word being rejected (v 128, 136)?*
- *Read verses 113, 115, 118-19. How does the writer feel about the people who reject God's word? What will become of them?*

But—didn't Jesus tell us to love our enemies? He did. Yet Romans 12:9 says, "Love must be sincere. Hate what is evil; cling to what is good." That is a very difficult tension for us to hold. Only in Jesus' heart can hatred for evil not be tainted by judgmentalism and hypocrisy. So how should we respond to this section?

Reread Psalm 119:136

We see sin and depravity being celebrated in society and used for entertainment on television. We see a loved one turn away from Christ. Of course we will feel distressed. We should weep at these things. But—first of all, and most of all, we need to learn to weep over our own hearts. The more you and I mourn the sin inside, the more we will be able to oppose the sin out there, without becoming judgmental.

It is never safe for us only to hate people. Jesus did tell us to love our enemies, hard though it is. But Jesus is the model who helps us as we seek to love what is pure and hate what is evil. He is utterly zealous for God's truth and condemns sin. However, in love he died for sinners like us—enemies of God whom he could justifiably have hated.

Pray

Pray that your heart would delight in God's ways more and more. Pray for humility and honesty to see the filth and ugliness that lurk in all of us. Pray that you would learn to hate your sin and to fight against it—for God's glory. Pray too that as you follow Jesus, you would be enabled to stand and speak against evil, without succumbing to judgmentalism and hypocrisy.

Bible in a year: 2 Samuel 1 – 2 • 1 Timothy 5

The missionary church

"Your mission, should you choose to accept it..." was the catchphrase of the Mission Impossible films. If you are a Christian, you have already accepted the mission of Jesus.

It comes automatically with being his follower!

Peace and joy

Read John 20:19-20

- *How did the disciples feel before Jesus appeared?*
- *What did Jesus give them and how did they respond?*

It is a wonderful change from fear to joy because of the peace Jesus gave. This is what he had promised (16:33).

Pray

Thank Jesus for peace with God, because his death paid for our sin and his resurrection proves it.

Mission

Read John 20:21-23

- *Why has Jesus given them peace (v 21)?*

This peace wasn't just to make the disciples feel better. Jesus was a man on a mission. He often spoke of the Father "who sent me". Now he sends all Christians on a mission. Of course, ours is not identical to his—but it is still a mission.

- *What equipping do we need (v 22)?*

This was not just for the apostles. There were others there (Luke 24:33). Besides, if it was just the apostles, Thomas would have missed out (John 20:24)! This is a promise for the whole church. It seems to be an acted picture of what would happen in reality 50 days later at Pentecost (Acts 2). Every real Christian receives the Spirit from Jesus to equip us for his mission.

- *What is this mission mainly about (John 20:23)?*

It is not about healing people or caring for the poor (though those are good and important things to do); it is about bringing forgiveness. This verse doesn't mean that some special Christians have authority to forgive sins. It means that all Christians can tell people how their sins can be forgiven, and warn them that there is no other way but faith in Jesus to find forgiveness.

TIME OUT

Read Luke 24:47; Acts 2:38; 4:12

Think about how the early Christians understood this mission. Did they go about forgiving people's sins? No, they declared the gospel in which forgiveness is promised to all who believe. It's about preaching the gospel of forgiveness in Christ.

Apply

- *Are you consciously accepting this mission each day? Do you pray for and look for and welcome chances to tell people around you the gospel?*

Seeing and believing

"Doubting Thomas" is a phrase that has entered the English language, meaning someone who is—perhaps unreasonably—sceptical.

But is that picture of the original Doubting Thomas actually right?

Testimony not believed

Read John 20:24-25

- *What do the eye-witnesses say to Thomas?*

But Thomas' problem is that he wasn't there (v 24): he hasn't seen Jesus.

- *How does Thomas respond?*

It's hardly surprising, and I'm sure we'd have been the same.

Seeing is believing

Read John 20:26-28

- *What changes for Thomas?*
- *How does Jesus make it clear that he really died and he is really the same Jesus?*

TIME OUT

Only John among the Gospel writers mentions Jesus' "side" at this point.

Read John 19:34-37

Jesus' side was proof that he was really dead. Now Thomas needs to see that side alive to believe he's risen.

- *What does Thomas call Jesus (20:28)?*

He recognises now that Jesus is God himself, as John has already told us (1:1, 14, 18).

Thomas didn't stay doubting. He was humble enough to change his mind when he saw the evidence: and sensible enough to worship the risen Jesus as Lord and Saviour.

A surprising blessing

Read John 20:29

- *Who does Jesus say is blessed?*
- *Why is this surprising?*

Thomas, like John before him (v 8), has believed because he saw. But people who believe the evidence of the eye-witnesses will be blessed more than the apostles! If you're a Christian, that includes you!

We speak of giving our "testimony" as Christians. But what we really mean is telling our story of how we came to believe the eye-witness testimony of the apostles. We weren't there: but they were, they are trustworthy, and we believe what they taught and wrote for us in the New Testament.

Apply

- *How does what happened to Thomas encourage you in your faith?*
- *How does what Jesus said to Thomas encourage you in your faith?*

Evidence, faith, life

How do we get real and lasting life? Is it by material things, or pleasure… or through religion, or some mystical path? None of these! The way to life is much simpler.

Evidence

Read John 20:30

John has selected just a few of Jesus' miracles. He calls them "signs" because they are signposts pointing to who Jesus is and what he came to bring.

TIME OUT

John's Gospel is sometimes called "The Book of the Signs". Flick through John 1 – 12 to see which miracles John has selected.

- *Which would you say is the biggest?*
- *Why do you think John has selected these particular ones?*

Faith

Read John 20:31

- *Why does John record the "signs" of Jesus?*

Notice that it's not just that he wants us to be "people of faith". The world talks of "faith" as if it is a subjective quality that some people have and others don't ("I envy you your faith," they may say). No! It is believing something specific.

What? The "Messiah" means God's anointed King, who will rule the world. We are to believe that Jesus of Nazareth is this King. Also, "the Son of God" means God himself, in eternal fellowship with his Father (see 1:18).

Life

- *What happens when men and women believe in their minds and their hearts that Jesus is God's King and God's Son?*

"Life" is shorthand for "eternal life", which means "the life of the age to come"—not life in heaven, but life reigning with Christ in his new creation, the new heavens and new earth.

- *What do you think "in his name" means?*

The "name" of Jesus stands for who he is and what he has done, especially what he has done for us on the cross. It is because of the cross that we, who deserve death, can be given life.

Pray

If you are a Christian, thank God that he has given you evidence about Jesus to believe. Pray for friends who are not believers, that they will look at the evidence and come to believe.

Business as not-quite-usual

Christ has risen! But what difference does that actually make to the lives of those who know and love that fact?

Business as usual

Read John 21:1-3

- *How many of the apostles are here?*
- *Where are they now?*
- *What are they doing?*

It's back to business as usual for these disciple-fishermen. (See 6:1).

Notice all the eye-witness detail John includes. Jesus had told them to go back to Galilee (Mark 14:28; 16:7). But the fishing is no good, which is probably a picture of fruitlessness without Jesus.

Better business

Read John 21:4-6

- *Who appears?*
- *What does he say?*
- *What happens?*

This must have reminded them of the incident in Luke 5:1-11, when Peter first met the Jesus who controls even the swarm of a shoal of fish.

It is the Lord!

Read John 21:7-9

- *How does Peter react?*

Probably he was stripped to a loincloth; before swimming he puts on his outer garment and tucks it in to swim. Then when he lands he can be properly dressed to greet Jesus.

Breakfast with Jesus

Read John 21:10-14

The number of fish doesn't seem to symbolise anything, but shows they counted and never forgot this wonderful catch.

But perhaps it also reminded them that Jesus had given them a new fishing job: to be "fishers of men" (Mark 1:17).

- *What does this third resurrection appearance in John show us about Jesus' body?*

Jesus may call us as his people to carry on with "business as usual": in the town we grew up in, in the same career as we've always been in, living a very normal life.

But with Jesus in our life, it can never really be business as usual! Jesus transforms our daily lives. He works through us to make a difference, and to further his mission to tell people they can have "life in his name" (John 20:31).

Apply

- *What difference will this make to how you view what you are doing in your days this week?*

Do you love me?

If you've ever let a friend down badly, you will know how awkward it can be to try to make up. How will they react? Can things ever be put right?

It must have been like that for Peter after his terrible denials of Jesus.

An awkward walk

Read John 21:15-17

Jesus and Peter have gone for a walk along the beach after breakfast (v 20).

? *What does Jesus ask, how does Peter reply, and what does Jesus then say?*

It's pretty much the same all three times.

In verse 15 "more than these" could mean, "do you love me more than these other disciples love me?", or "do you love me more than you love these other men?" Peter had denied Jesus three times both because he didn't love Jesus more than others did, and because he loved his own reputation and safety with others more than he loved Jesus. Now, Jesus lets him reaffirm three times that he really does love him.

Apply

? *How is this scene encouraging for us, as those who fail Jesus repeatedly?*

Notice that Jesus does not ask Peter, or us, to make up for our denials of him: but simply to come and walk with him in love once more. Through his death and resurrection, Jesus has already "made up for" our sinfulness.

? *What job does Jesus give Peter?*

It's a job of leading and of teaching.

A costly future

Read John 21:18-19

? *What is the contrast between Peter's past and future?*

The words "stretch out your hands" were used in the ancient world to mean crucifixion, where the victim's arms were stretched out and tied or nailed to the cross-bar. Peter's leadership in the church would cost him crucifixion.

? *Now that he knows this, what is the challenge for him (v 19)?*

Apply

This section reminds us of some crucial aspects of Christian leadership.

- The first qualification of a pastor is to love Jesus. Make sure you belong to a church where the leaders love Jesus.
- If you have any position of leadership in a church (such as teaching children, youth or a small group), remember that your first responsibility is to love Jesus.
- If you are in Christian leadership, remember you are not in it to become famous, popular, or rich. You are in it for costly service. It's a hard thing, and no one should do it out of selfish motives.

You, follow me!

The trouble with most of us Christians is that our focus is horizontal, not vertical. We mind more about others than we do about Jesus. Today we have a story that sums this up.

Three's a crowd

Read John 21:20

Imagine the scene. Jesus has taken Peter on that life-changing walk and Peter has reversed his threefold denial with a threefold affirmation that he loves Jesus. And Jesus has given him a privileged leadership job. But then Peter turns and sees John walking some way behind.

John calls himself "the disciple whom Jesus loved" in several places (from 13:23 onwards). This doesn't mean Jesus had favourites—but there was a close friendship. John knew him very well, which equipped him to write a Gospel.

What about him?

Read John 21:21-22

- *What does Peter ask Jesus?*
- *What might be going on in Peter's mind?*
- *What has Jesus just been talking to him about?*

Presumably he is wondering where John fits in to Jesus' plans for the future. Perhaps there are traces of a rivalry or jealousy: or perhaps Peter wants some reassurance that John will be with him.

Pray

Think about the ways in which we find ourselves asking Jesus, "What about him, or her?" and focusing our thoughts on the ministries, efforts, successes or failures of other Christians.

Pray that Jesus' answer: "You must follow me," will fill our ears and our hearts, so that we determine to follow him single-mindedly no matter what others do or don't do.

Error corrected

Read John 21:23

- *How had people misunderstood or misinterpreted what Jesus had just said to Peter?*
- *What did Jesus actually say?*

John wanted to make sure this was corrected before he died, to stop people being unsettled by his death—and to underline that what matters most is not what happens to other people but us following Jesus.

Apply

It is important to read the Bible carefully and see exactly what it says, and what it doesn't say. We ought not just to believe what we are told from the front in church, but to be people who go home and check in our Bibles that it's true. A friend of mine asks himself during the sermon, "Where did the preacher get that from?" It's a good question!

Truthful witness

It is a great thing to know you can trust a witness. Many a court case is decided on the evidence of a trustworthy witness.

It is even more important to know that we really can trust the Gospels. Today we finish John's Gospel with reasons to trust the author.

A witness we can trust

Read John 21:24

The disciple Jesus was talking about in verses 20-23 is the one who wrote down this Gospel. He calls it "testimony"; that is to say, the Gospel is John bearing witness that the things he says about Jesus are true. He assures us they are. The expression: "We know..." is a way of saying, "I can assure you..."

TIME OUT

Trace through the places where "the disciple Jesus loved" appears by reading **John 13:23; 19:26; 20:2; 21:24-25**. And he's there in **21:1-2** as one of the "sons of Zebedee".

- *What did he see?*
- *How well did he know Jesus?*
- *How does this give us great confidence in his Gospel?*

Many other things

Read John 21:25

- *What does John say at the start of the verse?*

It's an understatement really! Of course Jesus did many other wonderful things. We read about some of them in the other three Gospels, and there were plenty more. Wonderful miracles, marvellous teachings, glorious conversations with individuals.

John is not exaggerating here!

Read John 1:1-2

- *Who is this Jesus?*

He is the eternal "Word", the one through whom the universe came into being. He is the source and origin of all language, all rationality, all wisdom, all human thought and activity.

What he has done is more than Jesus of Nazareth physically did during his three decades on earth; it is the sum of all human knowledge and activity, the full story of human history, the amazing chronicle of the eternal providence of God from the creation of the universe to the end of time.

Writing down the glory of who he is and what he has done would require an infinite library!

Pray

Pause now, at the end of John's Gospel, to adore and bow in wonder before Jesus the eternal Word; and pray that you will worship him alone with all of your life.

EXODUS: Next chapter

The book of Exodus begins with the word "And". Our Bibles tend to miss it out, but it's crucial—it alerts us to the fact that this gripping story is part of a bigger story.

Read Exodus 1:1-7

- *Who do verses 1-5 introduce us to? How many of them were there (v 5)?*
- *What then happened (v 6-7)?*

The first nine words of Exodus are an exact repetition of Genesis 46:8: "These are the names of the sons of Israel". The book of Exodus is in many ways volume II of Genesis. The whole book needs to be read in light of what has gone before.

Read Genesis 12:1-7

- *What does God promise he will do for, and through, Abram and his family?*

The three key components, which we need to keep in mind throughout the book of Exodus, are...

- the promise of a people—Abram's family would become a great nation.
- the promise of a land—Abram's family would inherit Canaan.
- the promise of blessing—Abram's family would enjoy living in the way God designed them to, and through a "seed" from Abram's family, people throughout the world would enjoy that blessing.

Four hundred years before the events of Exodus 1, these promises were under threat—it looked as though a famine would wipe out the family of Abram (now called Abraham). But God arranged things so that Joseph, a great-grandson of Abraham, became "prime minister" in Egypt, gathered grain in preparation for the famine, and extended relief to his father's family. They "went to Egypt ... each with his family" (Exodus 1:1).

- *So in Exodus 1:1-7, which of God's promises is being fulfilled? Which seem far distant?*

TIME OUT

Read Genesis 1:26-28

- *What similarity is there between God's command to humanity as he created them and what Israel is doing in Egypt (Exodus 1:7)?*

So what is happening at the beginning of Exodus is not only the beginning of God keeping his promises to Abraham but also the fulfilment of his commands to Adam. Where humanity has failed, Israel is starting to succeed. So far, so "very good" (Genesis 1:31).

Pray

Read Matthew 16:18

We too are people of a promise. To be a Christian is to be someone who stakes their life on the truth of God's promise.

Thank God for all his promises to you (perhaps a particular promise is especially precious to you today).

Ask him to work in your heart as you read through Exodus to give you greater confidence in all his promises to you.

Things turn ugly

God's people are fruitful and numerous; but God's people are far from home—living in Egypt, not in Canaan. And things are about to get much, much worse…

Oppression to genocide

Read Exodus 1:8-11

- *What does the new king—or "Pharaoh"—decide to do, and why?*
- *How are God's promises being threatened?*

Read Exodus 1:12-16

- *How are the king's plans thwarted, and how does he respond?*

Read Exodus 1:17-22

- *How are the king's plans thwarted once again, and how does he respond?*
- *Imagine you were an Israelite. How would you feel by verse 22?*
- *Do you think you would see God's promises as more precious or less reliable than previously?*

Standing against the tide

Reread Exodus 1:15-19

Don't underestimate the pressure the midwives were under or the risks involved in what they did.

- *So why did they act in this way (v 17)?*

In other words, they held God in higher awe than the ruler of the superpower of their day, and they so trusted him to keep to his plans that they were prepared to defy the plans of Pharaoh. Living in awe of God and with confidence that he will keep his promises is what enables us to act with courage and take risks to obey.

Don't miss that the midwives are rewarded with children, a sign of having a share in Israel's future. This blessing is a confirmation that God will keep his promises—these children are born at a time when newborn children are supposed to be killed (v 21-22).

Apply

The 17th-century Puritan William Gurnall wrote, "We fear men so much because we fear God so little."

- *Who, or what, do you find it easy to live in greater awe of than God? Why?*
- *How does the failure of Pharaoh's plans to extinguish Israel encourage you as you look at what is happening in the world today?*
- *In what ways are you being called to act in courageous obedience by trusting the promises of God?*

A baby in the Nile

Every time an Egyptian sees a Hebrew boy they don't just have permission to, but are commanded to, throw that baby into the River Nile. God's people face genocide.

Out of the water

Read Exodus 1:22 – 2:10

Don't miss the irony in what happens here.

- *Where were the Egyptians to throw Hebrew babies? Where is this baby placed, and rescued from?*
- *Who ordered the killing of the Hebrew babies? Who rescues this baby?*
- *Who ends up being paid to look after this child?*

In 1:10, Pharaoh had decided to "deal shrewdly" with the Israelites. But he is outwitted by four powerless women—the Hebrew midwives, and the mother and the sister of Moses—aided and abetted by his own daughter.

But behind all this we are meant to see the providential hand of God. His unseen guiding of the most specific of events results in Moses being kept safe in a place of violence and death, and then being raised as a Hebrew, but with all the privileges of Egypt (read Acts 7:22).

Even sin is a context in which God is at work, for he incorporates acts of sin into his purposes. That is what he is doing here (Exodus 2:10) in drawing out Moses, the future leader of his people; that is what he did when two other rulers opposed not his people but his own Son (Acts 4:27-28); and it's what he does in and around us still today as he works for our good in all things (Romans 8:28).

Apply

The writer is inviting us to see God's hand at work in Moses' life—and to seek to detect his hand at work in our own lives.

- *How does this change the way you are going to view the aspects of your life that are not as you would have chosen?*
- *How does this change the way you view God's promises to you?*

Out of the ark

The word basket (Exodus 2:3) is literally "ark". The only other time this word is used in the Bible is to describe Noah's ark.

- *What are the similarities between Noah's and Moses' experiences? (Read Genesis 6:11-22; 7:11-23; 8:13-17 if you need to and have time!)*

Noah was rescued by God to lead the recreation of his world. Moses is being rescued by God here to do something similar. But Pharaoh is trying to impede this creative fruitfulness—and so he sets himself on a collision course with God. Here, God has thwarted Pharaoh by rescuing Moses out of the water. Soon, God will utterly defeat Pharaoh by rescuing his whole people out of the water.

Coming home

Between 2:10 and 2:11, Moses grows up, enjoying a privileged upbringing even as his people face slavery, oppression and death.

Leaving Egypt

Read Exodus 2:11-15

- *Why does Moses have to flee Egypt?*
- *In what sense are his actions here more reflective of his Egyptian court upbringing than his Hebrew parentage?*

Moses won't liberate the people through human power or politics. It is God who will free them. And so Moses flees to Midian...

Living in Midian

Read Exodus 2:16-25

- *How does Moses settle down in Midian?*

Midian is home for Moses—real home. The Midianites were nomads who wandered around the Sinai Peninsula and Canaan—areas that were part of the land promised to Abraham. The way Moses finds his wife has echoes of the lives of his forefathers in the promised land (Genesis 24:15-17; 29:1-14). In leaving the only home he has ever known, Moses has come home. He is a member of God's people, living in God's promised land.

And Moses knows it. The name of his first son, Gershom, is better translated as "I have been a sojourner in a foreign land" (Exodus 2:22, ESV). The point is not that Moses has left home, but come home. Egypt was where he grew up, and Egypt was the place of great privilege, but he now sees it as a foreign country. God's land is where he belongs. He identifies as part of God's people, not as part of Egypt. **Read Hebrews 11:24-27.**

Apply

We face the same choices as Moses. Once we are converted, the land of our birth and upbringing becomes a foreign land to us. Now we are pilgrims heading for the promised land: heaven—our home.

So we have to choose. Which home will set our priorities and our behaviour, and define our standard of living? Will we choose the "pleasures of sin" and "treasures of Egypt"? Or will we choose "to be ill-treated along with the people of God"? Will we choose "disgrace for the sake of Christ"? There is the stark choice: will you live for pleasure and treasure, or will you live in disgrace?

- *How does this most challenge you? In what way might it liberate you?*

Pray

"He was looking ahead ... he persevered because he saw him who is invisible" (Hebrews 11:26-27).

Pray that this will be how you will live. Speak to God about ways you find it hard to live as part of his people, rather than part of this world. Pray for grace to change as you look forward to home with him.

The non-burning bush

The first two chapters of Exodus barely mentioned God's name. Israel seems to have all but forgotten God. But now God has remembered them (2:24).

Read Exodus 3:1-10

What Moses saw

- *Where is Moses, and what is strange about what he sees (v 1-3)?*
- *What is the explanation for the strange sight (v 5-6)?*
- *How does Moses respond (v 6)?*

A fire often draws you towards it, as this fire draws Moses (v 3). But equally, we instinctively keep our distance from fire, for we know that if we go too close, it will harm us. So perhaps God appears in this way to highlight this need for distance (a key theme in the book of Exodus, as we'll see, for example in 19:10-13 and 20-24). It's not clear why Moses must remove his sandals, except that it is a sign of "holy ground".

The point is this: what we will see of God's love and grace in Exodus does not take anything away from his holiness and glory. God is awful and terrible in the old meaning of those words—he evokes awe and terror. You don't treat him lightly. He is not your "mate". God is above us, and to stand in his presence would be to hide our faces (3:6).

What God said

- *What does God tell Moses he has done (v 7, 9)?*
- *What is he going to do now (v 8)?*

The God who is above us has come down to his people, to work wonders for his people. He has, as it were, rolled up his sleeves to get stuck into his people's story, by acting to keep his promises to them. Slavery in Egypt is not the end of the road for the Hebrews—"a land flowing with milk and honey" is (v 8). There will be a happy ending.

But for Moses, there is a sting in the tail...

- *What part will he play (v 10)?*

Apply

Most of us know what it is like to feel forgotten by God or when God seems far away. Well, God says, "I have seen ... I have heard ... I am concerned".

- *How do you need to hear that right now? What might stop you believing it is true?*

It's possible that sometimes we don't hear him saying these wonderful words of comfort and hope, because God is also saying, "I am sending you". In other words, often he intends you to be the solution to the problem.

- *Are you ready to hear that?*

Two questions

God has told Moses that Israel is to be rescued from slavery in Egypt, for life in a land of plenty. And the one whom God is sending to accomplish this is... Moses.

And Moses has a few questions about that!

Who am I?

Read Exodus 3:11-12

- *Why is Moses' question in verse 11 an understandable one?*

Who am I? It's a question our modern culture invites us to ask all the time. We can invent or reinvent ourselves almost on a daily basis. But—as with Moses—a task we feel unable to complete is often the moment for an uncomfortable questioning of who we are.

- *What's God's answer to Moses (v 12)?*

Moses does not need to have higher self-esteem; he needs a greater sense of God's presence. And so do we. God says to us, *You can walk through life with me. You can find your sense of confidence and self-worth in knowing that I am there for you, and here with you. I will be with you.*

Who are you?

Read Exodus 3:13-22

- *What does God tell Moses about himself in these verses?*
- *How does he repeat or extend his promises in these verses?*

The crucial verse—and one of the crucial verses of the whole Bible—is verse 14. God tells Moses his personal name: Yahweh (written as "LORD" in our English Bibles)—"I am who I am", or "I will be what I will be". What does this name mean?

1. God is utterly sovereign. He is not constrained by anything outside himself, but he is constrained by himself (he is who he is). So Moses, and we, can be sure that when he makes a promise, he will keep it. There is no "maybe" attached when God says he will do something.
2. God is personal. He is known by his people by name, and his name means he is committed to his people. It's the difference between a person calling someone "Professor" (a title), because they have a professional relationship with them, and "Steve" (a name), because they have a personal relationship.
3. God is known by his acts. The "sign" of who God is is that Israel "will worship ... on this mountain" (v 12). God is self-defining, and he is about to provide us with a definition of his name—and that definition is the Exodus.

Apply

- *Why is it so attractive to seek to define who God is for ourselves? Why is that also so dangerous?*
- *Reflect on what you've seen of who God is. How does it motivate you to find your confidence and self-worth today in his promise that "I will be with you"?*

Promises to pray about

Why on earth would God help me and you? Why would he hear and answer our prayers? This section is a wonderful model of confident, faith-fuelled prayers.

The writer of Psalm 119 prays on the basis of who God is and what he has promised to do. God's character and God's promises are the steps on the stairway that lead us to the throne of grace in heaven.

Far and near

Read Psalm 119:145-152

- *What sense do verses 145-148 give us of the writer's life?*

His cries are urgent and desperate.

- *How serious is the situation, and where is comfort to be found (v 150-151)?*

"Meditate..." Psalm 119 is full of calls to meditate (v 148, for example). Meditation is not a weird, mystical thing. It simply means to chew something over. We all do it. We replay conversations or arguments, dwelling on the things people have said to us. We think about things we want, imagining what it would be like to have them. The question is not whether we meditate, but *on what* we meditate; and Psalm 119 encourages us to meditate on—to chew over—God's life-giving word and his trustworthy promises.

Apply

Take a phrase from today's psalm and screenshot it or scribble it down. Then think on it and pray over it whenever you have a moment today. Chewing over past arguments or disappointments leads to bitterness. Meditating on God's word brings freedom, life and joy.

Praying the promises

Read Psalm 119:149-160

- *What request is repeated?*
- *What reason is given for God to answer?*

God says that he preserves our lives "according to [his] promise" (v 154).

- *So why is the truth contained in verses 152 and 160 so important for our confidence and hope?*

Apply

- *Which particular promises of God or aspects of his character do you need to lay hold of today?*
  - *His compassion to forgive sins (Psalm 103:8-12)?*
  - *His promise to provide for your needs (Philippians 4:19)?*
  - *His help when we face temptation (Hebrews 4:15-16)?*
  - *Something else?*

Pray

Lay hold of those promises as you pray to God today. Thank him for them, and ask for strength and courage to live in light of their eternal trustworthiness.

I just don't want to

Here's what Moses is to tell the enslaved Hebrews: God says he's going to rescue you from Pharaoh, take you to a good land, and let you plunder the Egyptians...

Read Exodus 4:1

- *Why is Moses' question unsurprising?*

Signs

Read Exodus 4:2-9

- *What three signs does God offer Moses to establish his credibility?*

These signs will also be the first ones "performed" for the Egyptians (7:8-24). The third one will be the first plague. So what Moses will do to prove God's plan to Israel is just a preview of the greater signs—the judgment and salvation of the Exodus itself.

So it is for us. Jesus did many miracles, but they weren't tricks, to wow people; they were signs to establish his credibility, and previews of the greater, ultimate signs—the cross and resurrection (Matthew 12:38-40). These two events are all we (or anyone) need to show us the power and the wisdom of God.

Speech

Read Exodus 4:10-31

- *What is Moses' next objection to taking on his task (v 10)?*
- *How does God respond (v 11-12)?*
- *How does verse 12 reveal what lies behind all Moses' questions and objections?*

For all of us, there comes a time when we have no good reason not to obey, and all that prevents us is our own unwillingness to step up; and God says, "Now go" (v 12).

- *How do the Israelite elders react to Moses' message (v 29-31)?*
- *So far, so good... but what has God promised will happen next (v 21-23)?*

TIME OUT

Verses 24-26 relate a strange episode which raises questions which we can't readily answer 3,000 years on. But bear in mind that God has just drawn a line between the firstborn of God and the firstborn of Egypt (v 22-23). The firstborn of Egypt will die because of Egypt's refusal to liberate the firstborn of God. So the line is stark—between grace and life, and judgment and death. And circumcision was the sign that someone was part of Israel, God's firstborn (Genesis 17). In not circumcising Gershom, Moses was treating him as an Egyptian, and not a member of God's people. God's attack anticipates his attack on Pharaoh and Egypt. The only hope is to cross the line, to enter God's people—which is what Zipporah does when she circumcises Gershom. Today, baptism is the sign that you have crossed the line and are part of God's "firstborn son"—his people—united to his eternal Son, Jesus.

Apply

- *Is there a way in which God is saying to you, "Now go"? Will you go, knowing it will be hard, but he will be with you?*

Pharaoh's response

If a restaurant is full, say you're booking in the name "Tim Chester"... and it will make no difference! Say you're booking for "Beyoncé", and space gets found!

A name represents a person—and some names can open any door. They demand instant respect. Others don't. We see the same sort of thing throughout Exodus 5 – 6.

Who is this?

Read Exodus 5:1-2

- *Whose name do Moses and Aaron refer to (v 1)? What is his message?*
- *How does Pharaoh respond? Why won't he let Israel go (v 2)?*

Pharaoh is saying, *Who is this Yahweh? I've never heard of him. Why should I obey him?* After all, he is Pharaoh, the supreme ruler over a vast empire with almost unprecedented power. He is not in the habit of letting other people tell him what to do. Verse 2 is a declaration of defiance. The name Yahweh opens no doors in Pharaoh's palace.

Pharaoh's question is setting the agenda for the story of the Exodus, which runs through to chapter 14. Pharaoh asks, "Who is the LORD?" The plagues and Exodus will be God's response.

Make them work

Read Exodus 5:3-9

- *What warning do Moses and Aaron add in verse 3?*
- *What is Pharaoh's main concern, though (v 4-5)?*
- *What instructions does he give to the overseers of his Israelite slaves (v 6-9)?*

God wants Israel to rest more. Pharaoh says they must work more. God wants them to sacrifice to him. Pharaoh wants them to give everything to him. The issue is this: Who will Israel serve? And what will that experience of service be like for them?

In verse 9, Pharaoh portrays God as a liar. God has promised liberation, but Pharaoh says this is false hope: it is "lies"—lies because this is Egypt, and Pharaoh reigns in Egypt. The issue is this: Who will Israel trust? The ruler they can see, or the God they cannot?

Apply

Ultimately, whoever we work to please is the person we worship. Ask yourself:

- *Who am I trying to please?*
- *Whose approval do I most seek to gain?*
- *Whose disappointment do I fear when I fail?*

If the answer is not God, you are choosing to serve someone else rather than God. You are opting to be enslaved.

Disappointing start

- *How would you say Moses and Aaron's first meeting with Pharaoh has gone?*

Pharaoh has responded overwhelmingly negatively. Next, we see how Israel responds...

Hard to take

Things have got harder for God's people—so that the revelation of God's power will be all the clearer and more wonderful. But in the meantime things are still harder.

Made obnoxious

Read Exodus 5:10-21

- *How does Pharaoh respond to the Israelite overseers' request for mercy (v 15-18)?*

So next, the overseers speak to Moses and Aaron...

- *What is the tone of their comment in verse 21, would you say?*
- *What do they appear to wish had never happened?*

Not rescued at all

Next, Moses goes to speak with the Lord...

Read Exodus 5:22-23

- *What is the tone of his comment, would you say?*
- *What does he appear to wish had never happened?*

Israel do not really know the Lord. And so they don't trust him when his plans and his timings don't match theirs. Instead, they complain. Even Moses does. What does God's name mean? God's name means trouble, he says in verse 23.

While Pharaoh does not see why he should obey the Lord, Israel do not see that they can trust the Lord. By the end of chapter 14, both will have learned a lot!

It is this delay in the fulfilment of God's promises that reveals his people's hearts. When they were promised blessing, they were excited (4:29-31). But when they "realised they were in trouble", they started to complain about God (5:19). The delay tests them, and finds them wanting.

Apply

This is, of course, a challenge for us. See if this description matches you at all...

When you get what you want and life is going as you want, you're a passionate Christian. When God does not do what you want, when you want—when you realise you are in trouble in some way—you criticise or complain to God. When that happens, the true affections of your heart are revealed—that you love the blessings of Christ more than Christ himself. You trust him only when he gives you what you want but not when trouble comes—which means you don't really trust him at all.

How do we change? Lift your eyes to the cross. See God working good from evil. See his love and commitment to you as he gives you his only Son. As you do that, your affections will be rearranged, so that you love him, and trust him, and live with gratitude and not complaint, even in the hard times.

Pray

Pray through the issues that this study has revealed in your own life.

I am the LORD

Things have got harder for God's people now that God has got involved with his people. Their response is to complain—and now we come to God's response.

And his response is to keep promising and keep reminding Israel.

Read Exodus 6:1-8

- *What is the summary of God's promise (v 1)?*

Again, the battle lines are being drawn. Pharaoh said, "Who is the LORD, that I should obey him?" (5:2). God's answer is, *You will see. And then you will obey me.*

- *What both begins and ends God's speech in 6:2-8?*

Verse 3 seems to be saying that while God previously revealed himself in more generic terms (i.e. as "God"), now he is revealing himself in a personal way ("by my name the LORD"). But LORD—Yahweh—has been used often in Genesis (e.g. Genesis 2:4, 5, 7, 8, 9, 15, 16, 18, 19, 21, 22!). So more probably, God is about to give his name a new level of meaning through the Exodus. What he will do there will mean his people will know what it means for him to be "I AM WHO I AM".

So, what are we going to find out about what the LORD is like?

- *What has he done with his covenant—the binding promise he made to Abraham, Isaac and Jacob (Exodus 6:5)?*
- *What will happen when God and Pharaoh go up against each other (v 6)?*
- *What verbs does verse 6 use of what God will do for the Israelites?*
- *What relationship will he have with them (v 7-8)?*

God will keep his promises. God will be victorious over his enemies. God will bear all the cost necessary to free his people from slavery to Egypt, so they can enjoy a life of service to him. He is the promise-keeping, victorious, redeeming God. That's what it means that he is the LORD.

Read Exodus 6:9-30

- *How do the Israelites react to God promising them these things, and reminding them he is the LORD (v 9)?*
- *How does Moses himself respond (v 12, 30)?*

The point is this: they still do not really know God. If you are struggling to obey God, you don't need more willpower. You need to know God better. Exodus is a revelation of the name of God—the character of God—so that we might know him better, so that we might trust him more joyfully, so that we might obey him more fully.

Apply

- *Is there a Christian you know who is slumped in discouragement? How could you remind them of who God is, in a way that might both comfort them and challenge them?*

The plagues' purpose

We come now to the famous "plagues". The first nine take us through chapters 7 to 10, and we are going to look at them over three studies.

Then you will know…

Read Exodus 7:1-7

- *How does God lay out what is about to happen (v 3-5)?*
- *What is the purpose of the plagues (v 5)?*

It is not only Israel who need to know who God is. Egypt need to know he is the Lord too. The whole world does.

It's worth asking the question: why the first nine plagues? The tenth plague was the one that made the difference and saw God's people finally allowed to go. Why not skip straight to the tenth? Why all the bother and suffering of the first nine?

Read Exodus 9:14-16

- *What could God have done? Why didn't he, then?*

The ten plagues are a demonstration of his power. In this sense, they are missional. Their aim is that God's name might be proclaimed in all the earth.

Hard of heart

Scan-read Exodus 7:8 – 10:29

- *What do you see happening to Pharaoh's heart? Who is in charge of it?*

Three times we're told about Pharaoh's heart: that it "became hard", "was hard" and "was unyielding" (7:22; 8:19; 9:7). Three times we're told that Pharaoh "hardened his heart" (8:15, 32; 9:34). But it is also true that Pharaoh refused to listen because the Lord hardened Pharaoh's heart (9:12; 10:20, 27). We have to take both these perspectives seriously. Pharaoh determined Pharaoh's actions, and God determined his actions. Pharaoh freely chose to do what God had freely chosen that he would do.

Calamity after calamity is inflicted on Egypt, but Pharaoh refuses to submit. At one point his officials beg him to relent (10:7)—but he keeps on inviting more suffering on his country.

Apply

The hardening of our hearts overthrows reason. We find excuses for our sinful and proud desires. We find reasons for doing what we want to do. When it all unravels, we wade further into sin, rather than accepting our terrible mistake and backing away from it. That is what Pharaoh did. And that is why we need others to encourage us to fight sin, and expose for us the deceit of sin when we cannot see it for ourselves.

Read Hebrews 3:13

- *Who are you encouraging to fight sin?*
- *Who is encouraging you to?*

The Lord vs Egypt's gods

The plagues are a revelation of who God is, and a reminder of the folly of human sin, and today we see that they are a statement of the uniqueness of the only God.

Read Exodus 7:8-13

We're watching a contest between Moses and Aaron on one side, and Pharaoh and his wise men and sorcerers on the other.

- *Who scores first (v 10)?*
- *How does the other team match it (v 11-12)?*
- *Who wins (v 12b)?*

This is like an introductory unit to the plagues, which are the main curriculum. And the teaching point is clear: there is only one God.

In this "snake contest", more is going on than one supernaturally created snake eating another. Snakes were a fundamental part of Egyptian religion. In their belief system, the world was created by the sun-god, who took the form of a snake.

- *So what is represented by Aaron's staff-snake swallowing Pharaoh's magicians' staff-snakes?*

The plagues themselves are no different. As you read through them in a moment, remember that in Egyptian religious thought...

- Hapi, the Egyptian god of fertility, was closely associated with the Nile.
- Heqt, a fertility goddess, had the head of a frog.
- Apis the bull-god, another symbol of fertility, was worshipped at Memphis.
- Hathor, the goddess of love, had the head of a cow.
- Sekhmet was a lion-headed goddess of plagues, who could bring and take away illnesses.
- Nug was the sky goddess.
- Re, the sun-god, sailed through the celestial sea in a boat, descending each night into the netherworld but then always rising victorious with the dawn.

Scan-read Exodus 7:14 – 10:29

- *How is each plague a sign that the God of the Hebrews is more powerful not only than Pharaoh but than any of his gods?*

Read Exodus 7:22; 8:7, 18-19; 9:11; 10:7

- *How do the Egyptian religious leaders come to realise who the real God is?*

Apply

The point today is the same as the point then. Before our God, all other gods are powerless, all pretenders are defeated, all blasphemers are silenced. There is only one God, and he is the Lord. To worship a different god is to worship no god at all.

- *How does this change the way you see those around you who worship a god, but not God—the Lord Jesus Christ?*
- *How does this cause you to respond to someone who says, "I love that following Jesus works for you, but please don't impose your beliefs on me"?*

Seek your servant

The only person to have their own copy of God's law in the Old Testament was the king. Kings of Israel had to copy out God's law themselves (Deuteronomy 17:19-20).

Today, all of us can have our own copy of God's word. We can turn to it for guidance, encouragement and wisdom whenever we want. We can hear our Saviour's words of forgiveness and encouragement whenever we need. We can live like kings!

The final sections of Psalm 119 point us to the richest blessing of this royal privilege—God's word introduces us to God's Saviour.

Passionate devotion

Read Psalm 119:161-168

- *How would you describe the writer's emotions in these verses?*
- *What is his attitude to God's word?*
- *Why might we find these verses a little discouraging?*

May my...

Read Psalm 119:169-175

- *What does the writer ask for here?*

Pray

Pause to pray these things yourself right now.

Seek me, for I stray

Read Psalm 119:176

- *In what way is this an odd way to finish, given what the writer has been saying about his love for God's laws throughout this long psalm?!*
- *How does he describe himself? What is his great hope?*
- *Why is this a great encouragement for us?*

How very wonderful that God does not just send us his law to obey but also the true shepherd, Jesus, who came to seek those who had strayed, even at the cost of his own life (John 10:11-18).

We need Psalm 119:176—because otherwise the psalm can crush us as we read of the writer's devotion to God's word and feel like utter failures, knowing that we don't love it in this way. The final verse reminds us that this psalm, like the rest of the Bible, points us to Jesus. He is the true singer of this psalm, for he was perfectly devoted to God's law. He is also the Saviour who died for our failure to love God as we should. He paid for our sins, and he invites us as forgiven people to join him in discovering the delight of knowing God through his word. We live with the King, and like the King!

Pray

As we reach the end of Psalm 119, take time to write down all the things that you love about God's word. Then praise God for these things in your prayers. Finally, thank God that at the heart of his word is his Saviour, the shepherd who laid down his life for sinful, wandering sheep like you and me.

No other name

The plagues reveal the Lord as the all-powerful Judge—they also show him to be the richly merciful Saviour. And they point us forwards to Jesus, as we'll see today.

Scan-read Exodus 7:14 – 10:29

Judge

What role in the plagues is played by...

- *water?*
- *animals?*
- *death?*
- *light?*

Through the plagues, God is unravelling creation. Water no longer brings life. Animals no longer serve human beings—they invade like armies. Light returns to darkness. Life returns to dust in death. Egypt is "un-created". Pharaoh's world is a picture of life in meltdown under God's judgment. And God has warned us that judgment is coming. If we struggle to believe it, or to appreciate its seriousness, we must look at the plagues.

Saviour

What exceptions to the plague-suffering does God make (8:22-23; 9:4, 25-26; 10:23)?

It is only in judgment that mercy shines brightly. The darkness over the rest of Egypt was what made the light in Goshen, over the Israelites, remarkable and wonderful. Together, the plagues declare the uniqueness of God, both in his judgment and in his mercy. And it seems that people did come to know him through them. In 12:38 we read that a mixed group left Egypt—which means the plagues had acted for salvation as well as judgment.

Jesus

Just months after Jesus' ascension, the disciples Peter and John heal a lame man in Jerusalem and preach the gospel. As a result, they are arrested by the Jewish Council...

Read Acts 4:5-20

How is their question in verse 7 similar to Pharaoh's from Exodus 5:2?

What does Peter say they need to know about "the name of Jesus Christ" (Acts 4:10, 12)?

What strikes the council (v 13)?

The plagues were the revelation of the power, judgment and mercy of the character—the name—of the Lord. The cross and resurrection are the ultimate signs of these things—of the character and the name of the Lord Jesus. His name is the ultimate name. "There is no other name."

Apply

We are increasingly told to downplay, edit, update, or simply keep quiet about the uniqueness, the judgment and the salvation of Jesus Christ. But remember the plagues. When God goes head to head with the gods and ideologies of this world, ultimately there is only one winner. Peter and John proclaimed Jesus' name with courage because they knew there is no other name—that his judgment is coming and his salvation is available. We must proclaim Jesus' name too.

Bible in a year: 1 Chronicles 16 – 18 • Luke 2:1-24

The final showdown

Now we reach the climax of the showdown between Moses and Pharaoh; between the God of Israel and the gods of Egypt—the tenth plague.

Take a lamb

Read Exodus 11:1 – 12:20

- *What does God tell Moses to command the people to do in...*
  - *12:3-5?* • *12:6-7?* • *12:8-11?*
- *Why must they do this (v 12-13)?*

Notice that the Israelites face this terrible judgment of death just as much as the Egyptians. Israel are not innocent victims here, or they would not need to bother ensuring that a lamb died in their house so that their firstborn would not. They have to daub the blood on their doorposts precisely because they are as guilty as the Egyptians.

Read Exodus 12:21-28

- *How do the Israelites respond to Moses' command (v 27b-28)?*

Not a house

Read Exodus 12:29-30

In every home throughout Egypt and Goshen, the death count is the same. The following morning there is a corpse. The only question as everyone gets up in the night (v 30) is: Is it a lamb, or a child? Who has died? And for the Egyptians—for those who had not seen a lamb die in place of their child—"there was loud wailing". Don't miss the reality and horror of this. At some point after midnight, a lone voice could be heard in Egypt, lamenting the death of a beloved child. Soon that voice was joined by another. And then another. And the more voices that could be heard, the more people woke up to find their firstborn dead. "There was loud wailing." Those who had been bent on killing Israel's sons now had their sons taken from them.

The Lamb of God

The sacrifice of the lamb could only mean there was unfinished business—because how can a lamb be a fair exchange for a human life? The lamb was only ever a pointer...

Read John 1:29; 1 Corinthians 5:7; 1 Peter 1:18-19

- *How would you use the events of the tenth plague to explain what it means for Christ to be "our Passover lamb"?*

1 Peter 1:18 begins, "For you know..." He is saying that if we know that Christ is our redeeming lamb, we will live in the way he has just outlined.

Read 1 Peter 1:13-17

- *How do people who truly "know" about the "precious blood of Christ" live?*

Apply

- *How does the Passover in Exodus deepen your appreciation of your Passover lamb?*
- *How will you live differently as a result?*

Go, worship

Because of Pharaoh's hard and hardening heart, this was always going to be a contest to the death. And Exodus 12 is a chapter of death, in which there is only one winner.

Read Exodus 12:31-42

Promises kept

- *How does Pharaoh admit defeat (v 31-32)?*
- *How do the Egyptian people admit defeat (v 33)?*
- *What else do the Egyptians do for the Israelites (v 35-36)?*

About 600,000 men leave, plus women and children (v 37). Their numbers are swelled by "many other people" (v 38)—possibly some simply take advantage of the act of liberation, but perhaps others have come to share Israel's faith. After all, God had sent the plagues so "that my name might be proclaimed in all the earth" (9:16).

Read Exodus 3:10, 19-22; 4:21-23; 7:2-5

- *To what extent has God kept his promises to his people?*

Read Genesis 15:12-16

- *How do the events of Exodus 12 mark God keeping a promise made to Abram?*

Apply

- *How does the Passover give you more confidence in God's promises to you?*

Freedom begun?

The Exodus is often seen as a movement from slavery to freedom. In fact, through the whole book, the only references to freedom come in the laws describing the circumstances in which an Israelite is to set free an Israelite slave (Exodus 21:2-11). The Exodus does not lead to freedom—quite the opposite.

In 12:31, Pharaoh releases the Israelites from slavery to him to "go, worship the LORD as you have requested". The word for "worship" is the same word as the word used to described the slavery of Israel under the Egyptians (e.g. 2:23).

All along, we have been presented with competing claims to the service of Israel. To whom does Israel belong? Both God and Pharaoh lay claim to Israel, though the nature of their respective rules is very different. Under Pharaoh's rule the Israelites experienced work without rest, the state-sponsored murder of children, interference in family life and the confiscation of property. In contrast, to serve God is to find true freedom. Exodus begins with Israel being forced to build for Pharaoh—as we'll see, it ends with them willingly building for God. True freedom is found in obeying God as his servants.

Apply

- *Identify a way in which you struggle with sin. How might this simple truth, that serving God is true freedom, liberate you to resist that temptation?*

Bible in a year: 1 Chronicles 22 – 24 • Luke 3

Memory days

Unsurprisingly, the Passover was to become the defining event in the identity of this newly formed nation; and it would remain the linchpin of their calendar.

Read Exodus 12:1-2, 14-20; 12:43 – 13:16

Passover then

- *How should the day of the Passover be remembered (13:3-7)?*
- *In what other way are the events to be commemorated (v 1-2, 11-13)?*
- *What needs to happen during all these commemorations (v 8, 14-16)?*

There are two festivals, commemorating the same event. The Passover starts on the 10th day of the month of Aviv and ends on the 14th day. The Feast of Unleavened Bread starts on the 14th day and ends on the 21st. The key day in both cases is the 14th, the day of liberation. Each festival reflects a different aspect of what took place. The Passover commemorates liberation from death; the Feast of Unleavened Bread, liberation from slavery.

The consecration of the firstborn is to remind Israel that they are God's firstborn—they belong to him.

The point of these acts is that the people do not merely remember, or observe; they participate. They ensure that their identity as God's people continues to be shaped by these foundational events, even as the generation who actually lived through them die. They ensure that the Exodus continues to be a living reality for God's people, central to the way they see themselves.

Passover now

Read Luke 22:7-20

- *How many times does Luke use the word "Passover"? Why so often, do you think?*
- *Where does Jesus focus in his words over the bread and wine of the Passover meal?*

We still commemorate the Passover today—we celebrate *the* Passover. And just as the Passover shaped the identity of the Israelites, so the Lord's Supper shapes our identity as Christians. We not only remember the story of the cross and resurrection. We enact and participate in its meaning and implications. It becomes our story and our identity, our living reality.

We need to remember who we are, and whose we are, by remembering the foundational events of God's people. This is why we have been given the Lord's Supper.

Apply

- *How will the Passover in Exodus shape how you approach the Lord's Supper, and where you focus your mind as you eat and drink?*

Pray

Thank God for Christ's cross and resurrection—and for the meal of remembrance he invites you to share in. Pray that you would never forget who you are.

Backs to the sea

Israel must have thought it was all over as they ate their unleavened bread on the road east, out of Egypt. If they thought that, they were wrong.

Caught in a trap

Read Exodus 13:17 – 14:9

- *Who led Israel? How (13:18, 21-22)?*
- *Where did he lead them to, and why (13:17-18; 14:1-4)?*

By 14:2, Israel appear to be caught in a trap—and it is a trap of the Lord's making. They have their backs to the Red Sea, with nowhere to go. As soon as they hear of it, Pharaoh and his officials regret their decision to let God's people go (v 5)—just as God had known they would (v 3). So now, Israel are caught between the advancing Egyptian army and the Red Sea (v 6-7, 9). By verse 9, the trap seems to have been shut.

TIME OUT

- *How does God leading Israel into a "trap" in order that he might show his own glory give us a helpful perspective on the difficulties of our own churches and lives?*

You will see deliverance

Read Exodus 14:10-12

How do the people react as they see Pharaoh and his army thundering towards them? Is this justified, do you think?

Read Exodus 14:13-14

- *What three things does Moses tell the people to do (two in verse 13, one in verse 14)?*
- *What does he promise them?*

We are often in just the same place as Israel are here. They are full of doubt and despair as their enemy advances invincibly (apparently). Maybe you, too, see your enemies of sin and judgment on the horizon, and you're afraid. How can you stand against them? What you left behind when you became a Christian suddenly looks very attractive, and so much easier.

So we need to hear these words...

Do not be afraid: The Lord has fought for us too. Our enemies are defeated because God fights for us. Christ has taken on sin and death, and given us the victory, whatever things may look like.

Stand firm: Our struggle is not against flesh and blood and chariots, but the world, our sinful natures and the devil (Ephesians 6:12; 2:1-2). And we have been given the armour that enables us to "stand [our] ground" (Ephesians 6:13). Our armour is the gospel. Satan says, *You cannot resist me.* We say, *No, I can—I am Christ's. I can and will stand firm.*

Be still: We leave what is not in our control, or under our responsibility, to God—we know that he is for us, and we stay still.

Apply

- *Do not be afraid. Stand firm. Be still. Which of these particularly speaks to you today?*

Path through the sea

Pharaoh's chariots are bearing down on the newly freed slaves. Their only hope is Moses' assurance that "the LORD will fight for you".

Through the sea

Read Exodus 14:15-31

- *What does God promise to do, and why (v 15-18)?*
- *How does God gain total victory for his people and over his enemies (v 19-28)?*
- *What do God's people see, and how do they respond (v 29-31)?*

TIME OUT

Some sceptical scholars have sought to explain away this episode in two ways:

1. *It was a natural phenomenon.* But verses 21-22 speak of two walls of water. This is not a high wind and a low tide.
2. *It was the Reed Sea, not the Red Sea.* The sea was shallow and full of reeds—the Israelites passed by on foot but the Egyptian chariots became stuck. Yet if the sea was shallow, why did the Egyptians drown?! If the chariots were stuck, why didn't the soldiers chase the slaves on foot?

Bigger and better

As with the plagues (and as in the time of Noah), God is "de-creating" in judgment—water and land un-separate, the opposite to what God did in Genesis 1. And God is rescuing his people through his judgment. And in all this, God is setting up a pattern...

Read Isaiah 43:16-19

- *What is God, through Isaiah, pointing Israel to, centuries later (v 16-17)?*
- *But then what does he tell them to do, and why (v 18-19)?*

God says, in effect, *Forget about that. I'm going to do it again—bigger and better.* And he did—in Jesus. So often in the Bible, water represents—indeed, is used in—judgment. When Jesus was baptised, he was immersed in water. In Mark 10:38, he described his death as a "baptism"—an immersion in water. Water is the symbol of judgment. The cross is the reality. At Calvary, the waters of judgment engulfed Jesus and he died. But on the third day Jesus rose again. God brought life out of death and salvation out of judgment. God brought his people through the waters of death in the person of his Son.

Imagine the walls of water collapsing in on one another, with people and horses being tossed about and dragged down into the depths. This is what Jesus stepped into at the cross. Jesus plunged into the chaos of the waters of judgment so that we can walk through on dry ground. Imagine the people of God standing safe on the shore, watching God's judgment unfold before their eyes. This is what we are doing as we watch, with the eyes of faith, God's Son hanging on the cross.

Pray

Reread the previous paragraph and praise the one who went through this for you.

To be a pilgrim

The next set of psalms (120–134) are "songs of ascent"—songs sung by pilgrims making their way to Jerusalem, to the temple where God dwelled.

And they are our pilgrim songs, too, for we are on our way to the city of God, the place where he dwells. We are "sojourners" (1 Peter 2:11, ESV), walking home to God. Sometimes, the walk is hard...

Read Psalm 120

- *How is the pilgrim feeling, and why (v 1-2, 5-7)?*

Meshek and Kedar (v 5) were areas far from Israel and far from one another (one to the north of Israel, the other to the south-east). They stand for the experience of the pilgrim who is walking towards God's presence, but is still surrounded by a world that does not know nor respect God (or his pilgrim). That, too, is the experience of the Christian today—we truly are, as Peter describes us, "sojourners and exiles". We are here, but we are not at home here. We are, as the saying goes, in the world but not of the world.

- *How are you experiencing the tension right now of being here but not belonging here?*
- *What temptations does that tension bring?*
- *Have you faced the challenge of others insisting on conflict, no matter how much you seek to speak with peace (Psalm 120:7)? How did it feel?*
- *Have you faced the challenge of being lied about by those around you (v 2)? How did it feel?*

The distressed pilgrim affirms that having called on the Lord, "he answers me" (v 1). Yet the Lord's answer is not to take the pilgrim out of the situation, nor to change the situation itself.

- *Where does the Holy Spirit point the pilgrim (v 3-4)? How is this an answer to the distress?*

God's justice may be offensive to those who have never experienced injustice. To those who are the victims of lies, deceit and relational war-mongers, God's justice is a prospect that soothes the pain. God cares about how those who live in Meshek and Kedar treat his pilgrim people. There is a reckoning for what goes on.

Apply

"Too long have I lived..." Don't let an experience of the brokenness of this world or the sinfulness of this world cause you to despair, nor to accept it, nor to join it. Speak to God, and walk on towards God. Sing this song of ascents as you climb the often-rocky path to your heavenly home.

- *How does this speak to your heart today?*
- *Could you share it with another pilgrim?*

Read Revelation 21:1-5 and 9-14 and pray with excited gratitude about the new Jerusalem towards which you are walking through this life.

Bible in a year: 2 Chronicles 4 – 6 • Luke 5:17-39

On the eastern shore

The Israelites are now, at last, free of Egypt. They stand on the eastern shore of the Red Sea, ready to journey to Sinai and then the promised land. But first, they sing.

Their song

Read Exodus 15:1-12

- *How would you describe the emotional tone of this song?*
- *How is God pictured here? How do these pictures fit with what we have seen him doing for his people in the Exodus?*

Perhaps the key phrase is verse 3: "The LORD is a warrior; the LORD is his name". "I will praise him" (v 2) is literally "I will decorate him", as in a solider being decorated for his courage. There are twelve references to "chariots" and twelve references to horses or horsemen in chapters 14 – 15. Israel faced cutting-edge military technology sweeping down on them and their children. But that Egyptian army was no match for the Lord: the Warrior.

Read Exodus 15:13-21

Until verse 12, the Israelites have been looking back at what God has done. Now they look forward to what God will do...

- *What do they trust him to do?*
- *Why do they sound so confident, do you think (remember what they have just been singing about)?*
- *Why is verse 18 a fitting end to the song?*
- *Why is verse 12 a fitting summary of the whole song?*

Your song

Read Revelation 15:1-4

God's people are again standing beside a sea, celebrating God's victory. Revelation 12 – 14 has pictured history as a prolonged battle between Christ and the dragon, or Satan—and now Christ has won. Tellingly, the song that the people of God sing is "the song of God's servant Moses and of the Lamb" (15:3). In Revelation 15 we are clearly looking over the whole of history, but the rescue of Exodus 14 is also in view. The point is the threat to God's people at the Red Sea was one manifestation of this war—and the defeat of the Egyptian army was therefore a sign of God's overall victory, won at the cross and the tomb. We have been judged in Christ, and saved in Christ. We have passed through the waters in him, and now we stand on the eastern shore, on our way home... and we sing.

Pray

Use Revelation 15:3-4 as the basis for prayers of praise.

Then memorise these two verses, and work out when you will sing them to yourself today.

Bitter is twisted

Grumbling is something we tend to think of others doing, not us. But let's be honest: most of us grumble some of the time, and many of us grumble most of the time.

In 15:22 – 17:7, we get three stories of grumbling. Today, we are looking at the first.

Read Exodus 15:22-27

Grumbling

- *How are these verses very different in tone from the song that came immediately before them?*
- *Why do the people grumble?*

In one sense, their grumbling seems understandable. They need water to drink! But remember what has just happened. The Israelites have been rescued from Egyptian slavery in the most dramatic fashion. They have seen the hand of God parting the Red Sea and defeating the Egyptian army. They have sung, "The LORD is my strength and my defence ... In your unfailing love you will lead the people you have redeemed" (v 2, 13). But all that was three days ago. Today they are hungry and they are grumbling. When we think of it like this, the grumbling that has replaced rejoicing and trusting is inexcusable.

But then think about your own life. Perhaps you sing of God's unfailing love on a Sunday morning. But three days later—or maybe three hours later—you are grumbling. Think of all the things that God has done for you. Think of all he has promised to you. But think, too, how easily you lose a sense of perspective. Think how much better you are at seeing what you do not have than what you do have. All we see is bitter water. All we see is our problem or lack. And so we say, "Marah"—my life is bitter.

Grace

- *How does God respond (v 25)?*
- *What does God promise (v 26)?*

Notice that Moses does not grumble. Instead, he "cried out to the LORD" (v 25). The story is an enacted promise. If we trust God and obey God, we will find he is the God "who heals you" (v 26)—just as he "healed" the bitter water.

This episode sets the pattern for the next two:

- Circumstances are difficult.
- The people grumble.
- God graciously provides what they need.

Pray

Speak to God about the things you often find yourself grumbling or complaining about. Cry out to him for your needs, and ask him for help to trust that he will give what you truly need. Ask him to enable you to look at the cross and empty tomb and walk with confidence, knowing he will provide.

Raining birds and bread

Israel has complained about God's plan and provision… God has graciously provided for his bitter people… and they then completely fail to learn the lesson.

Better in Egypt?

Read Exodus 15:27 – 16:3

- *Why do Israel not need to trust in God's provision while they are in Elim (15:27)?*
- *How do they respond once they do need God to provide, in the Desert of Sin (16:1-3)?*

The people are effectively telling God, *We wish you hadn't bothered rescuing us. We wish you'd left us as we were.* One of the characteristics of grumbling is that it often imagines idealised and unrealistic alternatives. In chapter 2, the people were groaning and crying out. Now, all of a sudden they think of Egypt as a wonderful place to live! The Egyptians slave drivers are forgotten. Indeed, they suggest it was God who oppressed them in Egypt ("if only we had died by the LORD's hand in Egypt", 16:3). And they claim God's intentions are malign ("you have brought us out ... to starve this entire assembly").

Trust issues

Read Exodus 16:4-36

- *How does God graciously provide for his people this time (v 4-8)?*
- *What further instructions does Moses give about collecting the heaven-sent manna (v 19, 22-24)?*
- *How do the people respond (v 20, 27)?*

Some of the people trust their efforts, their savings and their provision. They go to bed looking at the pot of manna saved for tomorrow and that makes them feel secure. But the next morning, it is full of maggots and has started to smell. There is no alternative but to trust that God will provide tomorrow.

The exception to this is the seventh day—and again, this is an invitation to trust God. But again, the people struggle to rely on him (v 27). One of the ways in which we demonstrate that our trust is in God is our ability to rest. We can rest because we are trusting God to provide. So if you can't rest—if you're always busy with your work or your family or your ministry—it is because you're not trusting God. You're trying to secure your own future or create your own identity or provide your own justification.

In the desert, God is schooling his people to trust him with daily trust. As a permanent reminder of this lesson, a jar of manna is "to be kept for the generations to come" (v 32-36). We have to learn to trust him every day. Hence the Lord's prayer: "Give us today our daily bread" (Matthew 6:11).

Apply

- *How do you need to learn the lesson of the manna today? What practical difference would a complete reliance on God's provision make to you?*

Strike the rock

The manna shows Israel that "the Lord who brought you out of Egypt" (16:6) is with them, looking after them. But still they will not learn—still they do not trust him...

Testing God

Read Exodus 17:1-4

- *What is the issue, again (v 1)?*
- *What is the response of the people, again (v 2-3)?*

In 15:25 and 16:4, we're told that God was testing Israel—revealing their true reliance. Here, the Israelites are testing God (17:2, 7). They are standing in judgment over him, as though they get to decide whether he is good and generous, or not.

This is why grumbling is a serious spiritual issue. It hardens our hearts. **Read Psalm 95:8-11** for God's reflections on these episodes in the wilderness. What started out as grumbling at Massah led to outright rebellion on the borders of the promised land—and none of them entered it. When we grumble—when we presume to judge God—we are in danger of facing God's judgment.

Striking God

Read Exodus 17:5-7

The choreography here is very significant. The Israelites have put God on trial through their grumbling. And so the courtroom is arranged. The representatives of Israel are on one side (v 5). God says, "I will stand there before you by the rock at Horeb" (v 6). So God is on the other side. In the middle is Moses with his staff—the staff that brought judgment on Egypt (v 5). So Moses is, as it were, the judge. All this takes place "in front of the people"—they are in the public gallery, so that everyone can see what happens.

Israel are guilty and deserve to be condemned. God is innocent and deserves to be vindicated. But God tells Moses, "Strike the rock"—the rock where God is standing (v 6). It is the most surprising moment. Moses brings down the rod of judgment on... God. And as a result, blessing flows to the people, as the water comes out from the rock to quench the people's thirst.

Read 1 Corinthians 10:4

- *Who is our "rock"?*

What happened at Massah was a picture of the cross, where Christ was struck in judgment so that we need not be, and so that we might now enjoy streams of blessing (John 7:38-39).

Apply

Read Romans 8:28-30

God is working for your good in all things today, to make you more like his Son.

- *When do you most struggle to believe this? How might that cause you to grumble?*
- *What would it look like to live in gratitude at that point?*
- *How will remembering that Christ is your rock enable you to do this?*

Hands lifted up

We now reach the first of many battles that Israel will fight before they settle in the promised land. But this is more than just a tribal squabble.

Read Exodus 17:8-16

Raising the staff

- *Who begins the hostilities (v 8)?*
- *Why is Israel able to win the battle (v 9-13)?*

This is often taken as being about prayer—but there is no reference to prayer anywhere! Moses does not hold up his hands in prayer, but in order to hold up the "staff of God" (v 9). This is the staff that struck Egypt in judgment (e.g. 7:15-19; 8:5-6), that parted and closed the Red Sea (14:16-17); and that now proclaims judgment on the Amalekites. This is how the story is explained in verses 14-16—the "banner" (v 15) is the staff—the judgment and salvation of God.

Raising hands

- *What does Moses say will now happen, and why (v 16)?*

It was not Moses who first lifted up hands. The Amalekites initiated this conflict (v 8). They lifted up their hands against Israel, and only then did God respond with his own uplifted hand—the hand of Moses, holding the staff—as a sign of his judgment. Note that the Amalekites lifted up their hands not against Israel so much as "against the throne of the LORD" (v 16). In other words, by opposing Israel, it was God they were fighting.

The sobering message of this story is this: when we lift up our hands against the throne of the Lord, he lifts up his hands against us. And God does not bring his hands down until judgment is complete.

This story leads to another hill and another man with his hands outstretched and another story of judgment. God's people are again liberated through the judgment of God. Their enemies are defeated. But there is an important difference. Moses spread out his hands to dispense judgment. Jesus spread out his hands to receive judgment.

TIME OUT

The enmity between Israel and Amalek is a running theme through the next centuries.

Read Numbers 14:25, 43, 45; Judges 6:3; 1 Samuel 15:1-8; 1 Chronicles 4:42-43

Even after this, it seems that Esther's nemesis, Haman the Agagite, who sought to have the Jews exterminated in exile, was named after the Amalekite king, Agag.

Pray

Thank God for his judgment and his salvation. And thank him for this picture of the Lord Jesus' cross, tucked away in this account of a long-forgotten battle. Pray that you would live in a way that takes both judgment and salvation seriously.

A climactic meal

Chapter 17 shows what the nations face because they lift their hands against God—judgment. Then chapter 18 comes as a wonderful contrast.

Read Exodus 18:1-27

Father-in-law

- *Who does verse 1 reintroduce us to?*

It seems that Moses' wife, Zipporah, has been "sent away" by Moses and has been living with her father and her two sons (v 2-4), perhaps for her own safety.

- *What does Moses tell Jethro (v 8)?*
- *How does Jethro respond (v 9-12)?*
- *How does Jethro show a different reaction of "the nations" to God and his people to the reaction we saw in the Amalekites?*

Don't rush past this moment. This is the climax of the Exodus. So far in the story we've had people treading on holy ground. We've had spectacular plagues of blood, frogs, gnats and hail. We've seen the death of every firstborn Egyptian. We've had pillars of cloud and fire connecting earth and sky. We've seen a road through the sea with walls of water on either side. We've had manna appearing from heaven.

But the climax of all this astonishing drama is a meal—a meal in the presence of God and to which the nations are invited. And this is the climax because this is what endures. The dramas come and go. They live on only in the memory. But the meal continues. The presence of God continues.

Apply

We did not stand at the foot of the cross or see the empty tomb; we did not watch Jesus calm the storm or raise Lazarus. We don't get miraculous signs every week—but we do get their goal: a meal in the presence of God and to which the nations are invited.

- *How does this excite you about sharing the Lord's Supper next time it is celebrated in your church?*

A nation under law

- *What does Jethro warn Moses about (v 17-18)?*
- *What does he advise him (v 20-22)?*

This story is about more than management practice. It is preparing Israel to be a nation governed by the rule of God's law, so that "all these people will go home satisfied" (v 23). It is a pointer to the necessity and the goodness of the law.

Apply

- *Do you always see God's law as something that will satisfy you as you obey it? Why/why not?*
- *What might change in your life if you truly believed that obedience to God would satisfy you?*

My help comes from...

This has been my favourite psalm since I heard it sung as a young Christian. It is a song for a pilgrim who needs help, about the God who is always ready to give that help.

Read Psalm 121

I lift up my eyes

- *Where does the pilgrim look, and what does he or she ask (v 1)?*

"The mountains" on the path towards Jerusalem were a hideout for robbers and thieves, through which the nervous pilgrim must pass. They were also places where idols were worshipped—idols that promised help with fertility, prosperity and security.

So the pilgrim may be looking at the shadows, worrying about being attacked and asking who will help them. Or they may be looking at the idol-shrines, wondering whether to join the worshippers seeking what they need from those "gods".

Either way, the question comes: in whom will I trust for the help I need when I am weak and in need?

- *What answer does the pilgrim provide (v 2)?*

In other words, *I will trust the one who made those mountains.* There is no thief he cannot thwart, and no idol whose empty promise is not truly fulfilled in him.

He will not slumber

- *What aspect of God's care for his people does the psalm emphasise in verses 3-7?*

Here is why (health issues apart) Christians sleep soundly. We have a God who does not snooze. We have a God whose eyes never droop, and whose eyes are never distracted. Enemies may surround us and idols may tempt us, but God is right here, with us. No harm will befall us except that which proves to be his chosen route towards his heavenly city. There will never be a moment, in all of eternity, that our God is not watching over us, helping us by giving us all that we need. After all, "he who did not spare his own Son, but gave him up for us all—how will he not also, along with him, graciously give us all things?" (Romans 8:32).

Apply

- *What fears or hopes keep you awake at night?*
- *What worries or attractions tend to dominate your thoughts and direct your steps by day?*
- *What will happen if you stop looking at those things, fix your eyes on the Lord, and say, "My help comes from the LORD, the Maker of heaven and earth"?*

Pray

Lord, helper of your people, thank you that you never sleep, and always care. Please take my eyes off my problems and away from those things that tempt me, and fix them on you, the Maker of heaven and earth. Amen.

In front of the mountain

Living under God's law satisfies his people (18:23). And living under God's law also displays God to those who are not his people.

Promises kept

Read Exodus 19:1-2

- *Read 3:11-12. Why is 19:1-2 hugely significant?*
- *What do these verses tell us about God's promises?*

Apply

- *Which promise of God in his word do you find hardest to believe?*
- *How might comparing 3:11-12 and 19:1-2 help you to truly believe that promise, and live in light of its truth?*

Identity given

Read Exodus 19:3-6

- *What has God already done (v 4)?*
- *What identity does God hold out to his people (v 5-6)? What do you think each description means?*

God is saying three things:

1. *Israel are God's treasured possession* (v 5). This phrase is used of a king's private treasury (1 Chronicles 29:3; Ecclesiastes 2:8). Israel are God's valued, precious possession.
2. *Israel are a kingdom of priests* (Exodus 19:6). The priests represented the Lord. The word "glory" is only used in Exodus of the Lord, with the significant exception of the high priest Aaron's garments (Exodus 28:2, 40, see ESV). In this sense, Aaron bore God's glory to the people. They could see Aaron and witness his glory there. The priests also represented Israel. Aaron's ephod carried stones representing the tribes of Israel (28:6-28). When he stood before God, Israel stood before God—when he presented the blood of the sacrifice which secured forgiveness, Israel presented it. As a priestly kingdom, Israel is to represent God to the world through mission, and represent the world to God through prayer. The world cannot see God, but the world can see Israel—and the church today—and should see his glory in them, and in us today.
3. *Israel are a holy nation* (19:6). They are to be holy as God is holy. God's people are to reflect God's distinctive character in their distinctive life so that the character of God is displayed to the nations. They are to be a light to the nations.

Apply

In **1 Peter 2:9-12**, the New Testament applies this missional identity of Old Testament Israel to the church.

- *Which aspect of the identity of the church today most excites you?*
- *How does your local church display these aspects of its identity, and what can you do individually to contribute to this?*

The arrival of the King

Israel have reached Sinai. Now they will receive God's law. But first, they need to get ready—get ready for God's arrival. We'll take two days to look at this passage.

There are three "characters" here—God, the people and Moses. We'll look at the first two today and the third tomorrow.

Read Exodus 19:9-25; 20:18-21

The Lord

- *Who is coming, and what will he do (19:9, 11)?*
- *What then happens (v 17-20)?*
- *What impression of God do we get from verses 17-20?*

God doesn't simply save the Israelites from slavery and death. He saves them for something. He saves them for relationship—a two-way relationship with speaking and listening. He saves them so they can enjoy his presence.

- *But what do God's people need to do to prepare for his presence (v 10-11, 15)?*
- *What warnings does God give (v 12-13, 21-24)?*

It's as if the holiness of God is nuclear. To approach a nuclear reactor, you need protective clothing, and even then you must not get too close. In the same way, to approach God the people need to be consecrated, and even then not come too close. God is a majestic, awesome King. Notice that Israel camp "in front of the mountain" (v 2). That's a strange phrase—mountains don't have fronts! But thrones do—and Israel are subjects, at the foot of the divine throne.

Sinai shows us that God wants a relationship with his people; and that he is dangerously holy. He cannot be approached lightly.

TIME OUT

- *What goes wrong in our view of God if we forget either his desire for relationship with his people, or his perfect holiness?*

The people

- *How do the people react to God's presence (v 16, 20:18-19)?*
- *Why does verse 20 sound an odd thing for Moses to say?!*

In effect Moses is saying, *Don't be afraid, but be afraid!* What he seems to be saying is, *Don't be afraid, because fear is the right response to God. You're doing the right thing. And this fear of God will keep you loyal to God.* The people who should really be afraid are those who feel no fear and so take God lightly. They should be afraid, for they are heading for disaster.

Pray

Thank God for his perfection, purity and holiness. Thank him that he is not a pygmy, pathetic god of our imagination, but the real God of dangerous holiness. Pray that you would live in awe of him, so that you would live in obedience to him. Thank him that in Christ, God has made a way for you to approach him in joy as well as in awe.

A tale of two mountains

Now we turn to the third main "character" in this scene—to Moses. In some ways this whole episode is set up to confirm his role.

Read Exodus 19:7-25; 20:19-21

That mountain

- *Why is God going to "come to you in a dense cloud" (19:9)?*

In a sense the point of the conversation between Moses and God (the full content of which we're not told) was simply that it happened at all—Moses is to be God's spokesman.

- *What do the people ask Moses to do (20:19)?*
- *So what did Moses do (v 21)?*

Moses is going to be the mediator between God and his people. He will approach God on their behalf. He will speak to God on their behalf. And he will hear from God on their behalf.

This role is confirmed by all the ups and downs in chapter 19 (19:3, 7, 8, 14, 20, 21, 25—bear in mind that Moses is around 80 years old at this point!). Moses is literally a go-between. He is constantly going between the people and God.

Read 1 Timothy 2:5

- *In what way is Moses' role at Sinai similar to Jesus' role for his people today?*

Our mountain

We live a long time past Sinai, and a long way from Sinai. What are we to make of all this? First, God has not changed. He still wants a relationship with his people; but he is also still holy. Second, people have not changed. We are still unholy by nature, and in need of being "consecrated"—made holy.

Read Hebrews 12:18-25

- *What are the differences between the mountain Israel came to meet with God at, and the "mountain" we meet with God at?*

Each Sunday, this is what we step into. By faith, we step into heaven, onto Mount Zion, and around us are thousands of angels (v 22) and all the Christians who have died, now made perfect (v 23). And we do this because we have a greater mediator than Moses—Jesus, who came from the top of the mountain to the bottom, and ascended back, having died to deal with our sin and make us able to dwell in God's presence with joy as well as fear.

- *What is the warning that goes with this wonderful truth (v 25)?*

Apply

- *How does putting Exodus 19 and Hebrews 12 alongside each other help you appreciate...*
  - *what you will be doing next time your church gathers?*
  - *what Jesus has done for you in his incarnation, death and ascension?*

God's law and you

We come now to the law. And immediately, we are faced with a huge, and difficult question: how do God's people today apply God's law to life today?

Two things need to be borne in mind:

1. These laws were given to people at a different time in a different culture. Many of them are designed for an agrarian economy. Some seem designed to avoid any confusion or contamination with Canaanite religions, which isn't an issue for us. Some laws are designed to accommodate the realities of life in a fallen world, in order to limit the harm caused by sin (e.g. laws about slavery and divorce—see Mark 10:2-9).
2. These laws were given at a different stage in the history of redemption. The "old covenant", made through blood under Moses' leadership (Exodus 24:1-3, 7) has given way to the "new covenant", made by Jesus' blood (Luke 22:20). This means, in short, that Jesus and the Spirit replace Moses and the law.

Read Romans 7:6; Galatians 5:22-23; 6:2

We are called to be Christ-like, not law-keepers. You can't codify patience or kindness or goodness; the Spirit grows in us virtues that cannot be created by even the best law. The Spirit now internalises the will of God in us, and empowers us to obey his will, in a way that the old covenant law never could.

So can we just dispose of God's law in the Old Testament? No. **Read Romans 15:4.** We may not have to obey the letter of the law, but the law still matters. It informs our understanding as Christians in three ways—one of which we'll think about now, and another two which we'll think through tomorrow.

The will of God

God is not arbitrary or changeable. So the whole of his law expresses his will, showing how his will applies in particular contexts.

Read Exodus 21:28-29

Most of us don't own bulls!

- *But what timeless aspects of the will of God do these laws express?*
- *How might they apply today?*

Read Exodus 20:1-17; Mark 12:28-31

- *What does Jesus say underlies all the commandments?*
- *How does each commandment reflect these two great summary statements of God's will for his people's lives?*

Apply

- *Do you tend to see God's law as restrictive or liberating? Why?*

Read James 1:25

God's law expresses his timeless will and shows us how we can be more like Christ.

- *How does this motivate you to obey him today, in areas you find hard?*

God's law and Jesus

The Old Testament law points us to God's will, and it is immensely precious for that. But there is more…

Read Exodus 20:1-17

Our need

- *What had God already done (v 2)?*
- *So what is the purpose of the law not, by implication?*

Read Romans 3:20-24

- *What does the law do (v 20)?*
- *What does the law "testify" to—that is, point us towards (v 21)?*

So, the law points us to our need for a Saviour. We have all embarked upon a deep-seated rebellion against God, and what the law does is expose that hidden rejection of God. Suppose a child hates their teacher. How would you know? You would know as soon as the teacher expresses their will in a rule and the child refuses to keep that rule. That's what would reveal the child's heart-hatred. In the same way, the law reveals the state of our hearts—and what it reveals is a rebellious attitude towards God.

His life

Read Matthew 5:17

- *What did Jesus not come to do? What did he come to do?*

What does it actually mean for Jesus to fulfil the law?! First, Jesus fulfils the law by embodying love for God and for others—he always obeyed God. Second, he fulfils it by satisfying the demands of the law. The law points us to our need for a Saviour—Jesus, having lived the perfect life, died to pay the penalty of the law in place of law-breakers.

Apply

Reread the commandments, using them as a checklist against which to assess your own life—in terms of your heart as well as your actions.

- *What does this reveal about you? How does that make you feel?*

You will never know forgiveness and freedom from sin until you face up to this reality—you are a law-breaker. Denial is no way forward and it is no way out. Some people are stuck in sin because they refuse to recognise that sin is the problem—that they are the problem.

Pray

Reread the commandments, using them as a checklist to assess Jesus' life. Think about whether and how he kept or broke each of the commandments.

Now reflect on how all that goodness and beauty is yours in Christ. He died so that he could give it to you.

- *How does considering this make you feel?*

Turn your reactions into prayers.

Bible in a year: 2 Chronicles 32 – 33 • Luke 11:1-28

Exodus reflections

We've covered some of the most fundamental chapters in Scripture, showing us who God is, who his people are, and how we live in light of that. It's time to reflect…

Who God is

Read Exodus 2:24-25; 3:5-17; 6:2-8; 19:16-24

- *What is God like?*
- *What aspects of God's character have you learned about for the first time—or been excited by for the first time in a while—as you've read Exodus 1 – 20?*

Who God's people are

Read Exodus 5:19-23; 14:29-31; 17:1-4

- *What have these chapters shown us God's people are like, both positively and negatively?*
- *How has looking at Israel's response to God helped you think clearly about your own response to him?*

How God works

Read Exodus 12:1-13; 14:15-28

- *How does God rescue his people?*
- *How have the Passover and the parting of the Red Sea increased your appreciation for the work of Jesus Christ?*

How we (should) respond

Read Exodus 14:29 – 15:18

- *How do God's people respond to being rescued by God, for a life of obedience to God?*
- *How can you apply this song to the death and resurrection of Jesus?*

Apply

- *How has Exodus 1 – 20…*
  - *given you greater awe of God?*
  - *given you greater love for God?*
  - *helped you to appreciate what it means to be part of God's people?*

Pray

Use your answers to the Apply section above to praise and pray to the God of the Exodus.

Reaching Jerusalem

Heaven is going to be unimaginably awesome. And as Chinatown in London provides a taste of China itself, so your church is a flavour of your future home.

Made it

Read Psalm 122:1-2

The weary pilgrims have reached their destination. The opposition (Psalm 120), and the danger and the temptations (Psalm 121) lie behind them. Their "feet are standing in your gates, Jerusalem" (Psalm 122:2).

Apply

Pause to enjoy the truth that one day, you will stand inside the gates of heaven, welcomed in by the Lord God himself, and you will think: *Made it*. What a moment that will be! Rejoice over the prospect now, as one day you will rejoice there, alongside all those who said, *Let's walk this path towards heaven together* (v 1).

Inside God's city

Read Psalm 122:3-5

- *What is Jerusalem like, do the pilgrims discover?*

A city built "closely compacted together" was a thriving city. And this city is united in praise to God: a praise that comes from the lips of all kinds of people—"the tribes of the LORD". Unity does not mean uniformity. In this city, everyone is fully themselves, and fully united in praising God.

Further, this is a city of justice (v 5), "which is a ruler's first duty and best gift" (Derek Kidner). Imagine that—a place where right is always done, good is always celebrated, and wisdom is always chosen.

Tasting heaven

Read Psalm 122:6-9

- *What does the pilgrim speaking here call their fellow pilgrims to pray for (v 6-7)?*
- *What do they commit to doing (v 9)?*

We can do this today—for though in one sense we have not yet arrived at Mount Zion and the eternal "Jerusalem" that God is preparing for all his people (Revelation 21 – 22), in another very real sense, we are already there...

Read Hebrews 12:22-24

Are you a member of "the church of the firstborn"? If you are, then when you meet with other members of that church, you are experiencing, and you are to contribute to experiencing, a foretaste of the city of the living God. "You have come" there (v 22), even as you walk together towards there.

Apply

- *How committed are you to seeking the prosperity (spiritually, rather than financially!) of your church? Does anything need to change?*
- *How are you going to contribute to your church being more and more a place of unity, praise, justice, peace and security?*

Bible in a year: Esther 1 – 2 • Luke 12:1-31

AMOS: The Lord roars

Can a God who really loves his children leave them without discipline? Is judgment just for outsiders?

Ordinary man

Read Amos 1:1 and 7:14-15

- *You have been asked to introduce Amos. What would you say?*
- *Is Amos a likely candidate for being a prophet, do you think? Why/why not?*

Ordinary time

At this time in history (around 750 BC), Israel is divided into two. In the south there is "Judah", consisting of two tribes (Judah and Benjamin) with Jerusalem (aka "Zion") as its capital. In the north there is "Israel", consisting of the other ten tribes, with Samaria as its capital. Antagonism exists between north and south. Amos comes from the south, but largely preaches to the north.

- *Who are the kings of the two kingdoms at this point?*

TIME OUT

These were flourishing days for the north. For more information about these two kings and their times, **read 2 Kings 14:23-29 and 2 Chronicles 26.**

Extraordinary message

Read Amos 1:2

Some background: (1) Mount Carmel is a place full of luxuriant growth in the north; and (2) lions roar over their prey (3:4).

- *Where is God roaring from?*
- *What will be the impact of his action?*

The people of Israel were in covenant with God—blessed by him as they lived in his land in obedience to him. But they had broken covenant. And God acted in judgment because he hates sin.

We Christians are also covenant people, bought with the blood of Christ, God's Son (Luke 22:20). How much more must God hate the sin that creeps back into our lives?

Apply

God's kindness is not an excuse for corruption.

- *Reflect on the ways you show contempt for the riches of God's kindness by sinning complacently.*
- *What is more important to you: living in relative prosperity, or in increasing obedience to your Lord?*

Pray

Confess the sins you reflected on in *Apply*.

Thank God for the unbreakable covenant he has established with us through his Son's death. Thank him that Jesus' death covers all your sins. Thank God for the book of Amos.

Ask him to excite, encourage and challenge you from it.

A sorry picture

Amos is a prophet to Israel—but, strangely, his first word is to the surrounding nations. And he paints an ugly picture of what is going on around Israel.

Read Amos 1:3 – 2:5

Numbers and patterns

- *List the common elements between each prophecy (look particularly at the start and end).*
- *Which nations mentioned are believers in the true God?*

Did you notice that there are seven nations on view? In the Bible, seven is the number used to represent wholeness or completeness. So, here is a complete, representative portrait of humanity.

"For three ... and for four..." is a way of saying something happened multiple times.

Common characteristics

Have a look at each individual nation that Amos has in his sights...

- *What is the key sin of this nation? Can you think of examples of similar sins in the world today?*
- *Who is this sin committed against?*
- *Ask yourself: is this sin present in my life?*
- *What characteristic of God is most evident?*

Here is a composite portrait of God and humanity. All humans...

- are related to God.
- are accountable to God.
- know what is good and bad.
- are inclined towards bad.

God is...

- patient, but will not hold off for ever.
- a judge who promises that rebels will be punished.

TIME OUT

Read Luke 24:45-49

- *Given the state of the nations as revealed in Amos, why are the words of the risen Jesus to his disciples here such good news?*

Pray

Pray for those you know who don't know God and stand under his judgment. Thank God for the forgiveness available in Jesus.

Amazing grace, awful sin

There's something particularly horrible about having a gift thrown back in your face. Yet that is exactly what God's people sometimes do with God's generous love for them.

Surprise! Another nation

Amos has a cunning strategy that he sometimes uses to sneak up on his readers. He tells his readers seven things. Because seven is a complete number, they think he has finished; then he adds one more, with a sting in the tail.

Read Amos 2:6-8

- *What nation is now in focus? Why is it particularly sad to find this nation in this list of sinful nations?*
- *What sorts of sins are highlighted?*
- *How many sins are listed? Why this number?*

Punishment

Read Amos 2:13-16

This was a time when the nation gloried in its wealth and power. God refers to both here: an overloaded cart will crush Israel; her warriors will be overcome.

Responding to God's kindness

Read Amos 2:9-11

Nazirites were men uniquely dedicated to God's service. They set an example to the people of how to live for the Lord. One outward sign of their devotion was never to touch alcohol.

- *What great kindnesses has God shown to Israel (v 9, 10, 11)?*

Read Amos 2:12

- *How did Israel corrupt his good gifts to them?*

Two of God's greatest gifts to us are his word and godly leadership. To take them and compromise them is a terrible abuse of God's kindness.

Apply

It is much easier for us to notice the sin of those outside God's people than for us to acknowledge and admit how those who call themselves his people are rejecting his loving rule.

Israel probably nodded along to 1:3 – 2:5, and would have wanted to ignore Amos' words to them.

- *How can you ensure you're as quick to see your own sinful flaws as you are those of others?*
- *If God were giving a report on your own church fellowship today, what would he praise? What would he challenge?*
- *What are you going to do about the challenges?*

Hearing hard things

Although God sometimes has hard things to say to his people, his plans are always for the good of his people (Micah 2:6-7).

So, let's hear him with thanks and a determination to amend our ways if and where we need to.

Gift and change

Read Amos 3:1-2

- *What privilege do God's people have?*
- *But what does their status not exempt them from?*

Covenants have two sides.

- God commits himself to those in covenant with him. He will bless his covenant people.
- God's people are to be faithful to God and obedient to his word. God's gift demands a change in our behaviour.

Apply

- *Are you someone who sometimes wants the gift of relationship with God but not the change in behaviour?*
- *How do these verses challenge you?*

Who can but speak?

Read Amos 3:3-8

- *What are the first seven causes and effects listed here (v 3-6)?*

In verse 8, fearing the lion's roar is linked to the right response to God's words.

- *So what should happen when God speaks?*

Pray

Just like Amos, we have been given God's word to declare to God's world (if you have time, **read 1 Peter 2:9-10**). It is part of being one of God's people.

Pray (and also plan) for opportunities to speak about Jesus to others.

Read Amos 3:9-15

God calls two pagan nations to witness his accusation against his people.

- *What is God's primary accusation against Israel (v 10)?*
- *What specific example is given?*
- *How will God's punishment of his people fit the crime (v 13-15)?*

God's generosity towards his people should be met by generosity from his people, but this is not how Israel acts.

Apply

We may not have a great deal of loot, nor great fortresses to store it in! But we can live out the opposite of verse 10, by seeking to do right; and by using our homes and possessions to be radically generous to others.

- *How could you do this more?*

Read 2 Corinthians 8:9

- *How is Jesus our example and inspiration in this way of life?*

Prepared to meet God?

Bashan was a plain where lush grasses abounded and where cattle were well fed, healthy, and even plump.

Hear this!

Read Amos 4:1-3

- *What are the women described as "cows of Bashan" like (v 1)?*
- *How does God respond to them (v 2-3)?*

TIME OUT

- *How do we see "cows of Bashan" in our society today? Do you see the same attitude in your own heart?*

Verse 2 is very unusual: God swears an oath by an attribute of his very own being, his holiness. This is an indication that the judgment promised is definitely going to happen.

Apply

Much of Amos is concerned with issues of social injustice. God clearly hates wealth that is self-focused and exploitative.

- *W're being prodded to ask ourselves: would God be pleased with my use of money? Does it reflect God's generosity to me?*

False worship

Read Amos 4:4-5

The first king of Israel, Jeroboam, built idolatrous religious sites at Shechem and Bethel (1 Kings 12:25-33). These sites were not endorsed by God, who lived among his people in the Jerusalem Temple. Amos is rebuking worship which pretends it is for God's glory, but is really about the glory of the worshipper.

- *How impressive would Israel's actions in Amos 4:4-5 have looked from the outside?*
- *How does God describe them (v 4)?*
- *What is the warning for us as Christians today?*

Past and present

Read Amos 4:6-11

Many of the curses listed here reflect the covenant curses of Leviticus 26, which God warned would come upon those who break covenant with God.

- *Which phrase is repeated throughout this passage?*
- *What does it imply about the goal of God's judgment on Israel?*

Read Amos 4:12-13

In verses 6-11, God sent seven natural disasters. Now he will send... himself.

- *Who is this God (v 13)? If you'd been there, how would you feel about meeting him?*

Apply

When Peter talks about the coming of the Lord Jesus as Judge, he urges that we "make certain the Lord finds you pure, spotless, and living at peace" (2 Peter 3:14, CEV).

- *What practical things might help you do this?*

Seek God and live!

The Bible starts with a picture of real life as God intends it to be. A life enjoying God's world, in unspoilt friendship with him. How can you and I find this sort of life?

Read Amos 5:1-17

Looking at patterns

There are lots of words and phrases here that repeat themselves or are similar to each other. It's helpful to look at the matching pairs.

- *What is the central idea of verses 4-6 that is repeated in verses 14-15?*
- *What does verse 7 say characterises Israel's life? How similar is this to the sentiment of verses 10-13?*

The central verses of this section of Amos appear to be verses 8-9, which is a sort of hymn about God, portraying him as the Creator (v 8) and Judge (v 9). He is the one who really matters.

Of course, if God is really the Creator and Judge, and sin is present in his world (v 7, 10-13), then justice will certainly be carried out (v 1-3, 16-17).

Seeking God

- *What must Israel stop doing (v 5)?*
- *What must Israel do instead (v 4, 6)?*

Reread Amos 5:14-15

Verses 14-15 are parallel to verses 4-6. They show us that seeking God in our hearts also means reflecting God's priorities in our lives.

- *What attitudes do "God-seekers" have?*
- *How is this different to Israel's practices (v 11-12)?*

TIME OUT

Read Mark 12:28-31

- *How are Jesus' words similar to God's words in Amos 5?*
- *How does Amos 5 help us to see what Jesus means we must not do, and what we must do, if we truly want to live as God's people?*
- *What would Amos 5:11-12 look like in your society? Are there ways you can get caught up in these things?*

Pray

Ask God to give you a heart which seeks to know, love and obey him. Ask him to give you a heart which shares his priorities—which loves your neighbour, and seeks to protect the vulnerable.

Talk to him about any ways this passage has particularly challenged you personally.

Subjects of ridicule

Psalm 122 took us to the gates of Jerusalem. Psalm 123 takes us back out to the road that leads there—a road that is so often painful.

Read Psalm 123

We have endured

- *What are these pilgrims experiencing at the hands of others (v 3-4)?*

"Contempt" leaves no physical marks, yet it wounds deeply and can leave lasting scars.

- *Why is that, do you think?*
- *So what are these pilgrims asking God to do when they say "Have mercy on us" (v 3)?*

Pray

- *Are you facing—or have you recently faced—serious contempt or ridicule from those around you, because you live as though heaven is real, and you belong there and not here?*
- *Do you need to bring it to God, and ask him for the mercy of relief?*

You sit enthroned

- *What does this pilgrim remind himself or herself about God (v 1)?*
- *What kind of relationship do they have with "the LORD our God" (v 2)?*

If you are a slave, everything depends on the character of your master. It is no bad thing to be the slave of a master who is always kind, loving and caring, and who gives of himself more than he asks of you. And that is the sort of master we can look towards, as slaves of the God who came to die for us.

Yet at the same time, if you are a slave, you don't get to demand anything from your master, nor insist that he hurries up. We look to God to ask for relief from our struggles—and then we wait. Sometimes, we wait for a long time. Waiting demonstrates trust and humility. And waiting gets its reward, for one day there will be relief for pilgrims and judgment of mockers (2 Thessalonians 1:4-10).

And, after all, when your eyes are fixed on the one who sits enthroned in heaven, and who is leading us home to be with him, the slings and arrows fired by those around you don't hurt so much.

Apply

- *Is the Lord asking you to wait awhile in some way? Can you see how the wait might be for your good, to build your trust in him or humility before him?*

While elsewhere in the world our brothers and sisters face far worse, in the Western world contempt and ridicule are common weapons deployed against God's people.

Read Acts 5:27-33, 41-42

- *Are you ready to respond to contempt or disgrace both with prayers to God for relief and with a joy that you get to stand up for his name?*

The sin God hates

Because he's loving and just, God hates all sin. But this passage introduces us to a surprising, and challenging, way of sinning which God despises.

I despise your…

Read Amos 5:21-27

- *What does God hate (v 21)? What will he not accept (v 22)?*
- *What is shocking about this?*
- *What is really at the centre of Israel's religious life and devotion (v 26)?*

Notice how often "you" and "your" occur. It's been the problem with humanity since Genesis 3. We take even the most sacred things and turn them into something that has us, our desires and gratification, at the centre.

Apply

- *How is this a challenging reminder to people who are religious or churchgoing?*

Pray

Pray that the focus of your church life would truly be the Lord Jesus, and not us. Pray for leaders whose focus is exalting Jesus.

Pampered people

Read Amos 6:1-7

- *What signs are there here that these are a people who are "full of themselves"?*

TIME OUT

- *Why do you think that often the poor are rich in faith whereas the rich are not?*

The root of the problem

Read Amos 6:8-14

- *What sin, which God really hates, lies at the heart of what Israel is doing (v 8)?*

It is this that underlies Israel's religious practice (5:21-27), use of wealth (6:1-7), and feeling of self-sufficiency (v 13).

Not the day you expected

Read Amos 5:18-20

"Woe" is shorthand for: "God's judgment is coming".

- *What is surprising about verse 18?*
- *How has today's passage shown us why Israel, despite being God's people, had no reason to look forward to his coming?*

When the Lord comes, human pride will be shattered. Those who think they don't need God or who assume God will accept them, will not enjoy his coming.

Apply

Read Acts 17:31

The only way to be prepared for the day of the Lord is to humble ourselves, give up our pride and self-reliance and ask Jesus to be our Saviour as well as our Judge.

- *Are you ready?*

Without hope?

Can we ever be beyond the reach of God's grace?

Two visions

Read Amos 7:1-6

Chapters 7 – 9 are structured around five visions. Keep an eye on these visions; they shape the rest of the message of Amos.

- *Find the similarities in pattern between vision one (v 1-3) and vision two (v 4-6).*
- *Are there any differences that strike you (e.g. in wording or message)?*

TIME OUT

Read Deuteronomy 7:6-8

Amos, unlike the rest of Israel (Amos 6:13), is willing to see Israel in the same way God does—as small and insignificant.

Visions three and four

Read Amos 7:7-9 and 8:1-3

Find the similarities in pattern between vision three (7:7-9) and vision four (8:1-3).

- *Are there any differences between these two visions, and the previous ones?*

The crucial difference: in the second set, Amos does not intercede, and God does not relent. It is clear that God has now had enough; his patience has run out.

This prophecy is directed towards God's people, who have treated God's patience with scorn. Like all humans, their sinfulness has corrupted everything, leaving God angry and us with nowhere to hide.

- *What troubling image does God leave us with (8:3)? What sound is there?*

God's judgment is too terrible for words.

Death to life

Read Ephesians 2:1-10

Paul is writing to a church—but in verses 1-3, he's describing the position of these people before they turned to Jesus as their Lord.

- *What were they (v 1)? What were they facing (v 3)?*
- *What are they now (v 5)?*
- *How has this happened (v 4-6, 8)?*

The great news of the gospel is there is a place to hide from judgment: Christ. God has mercy on those who deserve his judgment but put their faith in his Son.

Pray

Thank God for showing us the awfulness of his judgment, so that we would run to Jesus for forgiveness. Try to find some words to say thank you: though of course an awed, grateful silence will do!

Pray for your friends and family who do not know Christ. List them. Ask God to turn them to put their faith in Jesus, so that they might be "made alive".

Much obliged

All of us are people under obligation or duty. Here, we meet two people who have a duty, and who respond to their obligations very differently.

Amaziah

Priests had at least two roles: to speak God's word, and mediate his forgiveness.

Read Amos 7:10-13

- *Who is Amaziah?*
- *What charges does he put before the king?*

Amaziah fails to fulfil his obligations and protects himself by (1) focusing on political matters and (2) omitting the religious basis of Amos' words and his charges against the false sanctuaries and their practices.

How do his words in verse 12 fall short of fulfilling God's obligations for a priest?

Apply

We hear the word of God regularly: in church, in Bible-study groups, as we use *Explore*. And we always face a choice about what to do with what we read.

- *Hearing God's word is a serious business. Think back to last Sunday's sermon. Assuming it was clearly based on the Bible, how are you responding to it this week?*
- *Think back to the last month or so of Explore studies. What has changed in your attitudes or actions as a result of what you've read in God's word?*

Amos

Read Amos 7:14-17

- *Why do you think Amos says that he was no prophet or prophet's son?*
- *So what are Amos' credentials for being a prophet?*

Amos faced two commands: one from a human with great status and power, and one from God. The human commands silence; God commands speech.

- *What does verse 16 show us about who Amos will obey?*

TIME OUT

Read Acts 4:5-6, 18-20

- *How did Peter and John face the same choice as Amos? Which did they choose?*
- *How does this inspire and challenge you?*

Us

We have the privilege, and obligation, of speaking about the great thing God has done for the world in Jesus (1 Peter 2:9-12). We will face a world which would rather we kept quiet, and will sometimes resort to taunts, threats or worse to get what they want.

Apply

- *Who has God given you the opportunity—and obligation—to speak to about the Lord Jesus?*

Bible in a year: Joshua 16 – 18 • Luke 17:20-37

Darkness and silence

What is the worst thing that could happen to you? What is the one thing in your life which you would least like God to remove?

Why?

Read Amos 8:1-6

Both New Moon and Sabbath were times of rest—not working. So in Israel, these were "non-profit" days.

- *What reasons do verses 4-6 give for God's judgment, which he announced in verses 1-3?*
- *What would these sins look like today?*
- *Who suffers the most as a result of the activities outlined here?*

Apply

We may not be guilty of the sins outlined here. However, neglect or abuse of the disadvantaged is close to the door of such sins.

- *Does your heart long for the spiritually and physically disadvantaged, as God's heart does?*

What?

Read Amos 8:7-14

- *List the judgments promised by God:* *•v 7 •v 9 •v 10 •v 11-14*
- *Of these, which seems to be the worst? Why?*

TIME OUT

Read Deuteronomy 8:3

Without a word from God there is no guidance, no comfort, no promise and, worst of all, no access to God. When God is silent, all is lost.

God's ultimate word

Read John 1:1-5, 14

The great news is that God, in his mercy, has not left the world without his word. He has spoken clearly, definitively and powerfully through his Word made flesh; through the person of his Son.

Apply

"These are the ones I look on with favour: those who are humble and contrite in spirit, and who tremble at my word." (Isaiah 66:2).

- *How are you doing at "trembling" in awe and respect at God's word?*
- *What practical differences does, or would, trembling at God's word make to you?*

Pray

Pray that God will help you to be a person who trembles at his Word, the awesome Lord Jesus, as you read his words in the Bible.

No escape

We now turn to Amos' fifth vision. If Israel had any illusions about God's intentions, any thought that they might escape, they are shattered here.

No escape

Read Amos 9:1-4

- *What is coming? How do you feel about this?*
- *What have we seen in Amos so far which shows the judgment of God is deserved?*

The altar was a place of refuge and grace—the place people could come to make sacrifices to God and be assured of his favour towards them.

- *So why are these verses particularly shocking?*

TIME OUT

We normally think of the truths that God is always with us, and knows us intimately, as comforting and encouraging. But the fact that God knows everything about us is deeply unsettling too. It means we cannot hide our sin. And it means we cannot hide from him.

Pray

We can hide our sin from others, and sometimes even from ourselves—but not from God. So spend some time now being honest with him.

Declaring God's power

Read Amos 9:5-6

Throughout Amos there are a number of outbursts of praise to God the Creator, often in the midst of strong statements of judgment. Why? Perhaps it is because God's power over creation demonstrates his right and ability to carry out his judgments.

Pray

Use verses 5-6 as the basis of praise to God the Creator.

No escape

Read Amos 9:7-10

- *If Israel thought that their special status with God protected them, with what arguments does God respond?*
- *What note of hope is there in verse 8?*

Pray

It's easy to think that there ought to be less judgment, and more hope, in Old Testament prophets such as Amos! But in fact, by rights there would be more judgment, and no hope. Judgment is all that sinful people deserve: hope is a gift from God.

So thank him that he offers hope to sinners. Ask him to help you feel the force of his promise of judgment, so you cling all the more tightly to the forgiveness Jesus won for you at the cross.

Blood and lavender

As one commentator puts it, everything up to this point has been blood and iron, but these verses are lavender.

Given the stench of sin in the book, it is wonderful—and a relief!—to smell the sweet smell of grace.

Restoration

Read Amos 9:11-12

- *What is God going to do for Israel?*

David, the greatest king of Israel, was a "man after [God's] own heart" (1 Samuel 13:14).

- *How does that help us to see how great Amos 9:11 is?*
- *Why can we be confident this will happen (v 12)?*

A sure word

Read Amos 9:13-15

Up until now, when God has spoken about the future days or "day of the LORD", he has promised darkness and punishment.

- *What kind of days does he speak of now?*
- *What picture of life is being painted?*

Notice that this is all God's work. "I will..." (v 14); "I will..." (v 15). They will enjoy life in the land "I have given them" (v 15). It will not be Israel's effort that achieves this blessed life—it will be God's grace and power.

But...

How can God move from the blood and iron of deserved punishment to the lavender of blessing? How can Amos promise both that judgment is coming, and that salvation is coming?

Read Romans 3:21-26

- *How do God's judgment and his mercy meet at the cross?*

Only in and because of Jesus can God be as we see him in Amos 9:11-15. But because of Jesus, the days we can look forward to as his people are, wonderfully, the days these verses describe. The day of judgment need hold no terror for us.

Apply

How should we respond to this? Here are three suggestions:

- Thankfulness: we should be overwhelmed with gratitude and thanks.
- Repentance: we should turn back from the sin that required the death of Jesus.
- Love: we should love as we are loved.

- *What would change in your life if it were filled with these three qualities?*

Pray

Thank God for the book of Amos. Thank him for telling us what we need to hear, not what we'd like to hear. And ask him to fill your heart and life with thankfulness, repentance and love.

But he is

This psalm invites us to think the unthinkable: what if God weren't on his people's side? In doing so, it moves us to celebrate the great, immovable truth: but he is.

Read Psalm 124

David and the pilgrims

David, the writer, is imagining what would have happened if the Lord had not been on his side...

- *What four images does he use?*
  - *v 3*
  - *v 4-5*
  - *v 6*
  - *v 7*
- *What impression do these give of...*
  - *how serious the danger was?*
  - *how close he came to defeat?*
- *How does meditating on this situation and God's rescue of him give him confidence in the present (v 8)?*

We can't know for sure, but some commentators think David penned this psalm in the face of the repeated and apparently overwhelming torrents of Philistine attacks at the very start of his reign (2 Samuel 5:17-25). What is striking, though, is that it was later adopted by pilgrims (members of Israel), and not only its monarch, as a "song of ascents" (introduction to Psalm 124). It is inviting the ordinary believer to see that this deliverance of and reliance upon the Lord is the experience both of the king of God's people and of each one of God's people.

Jesus and us

And so we today are invited to meditate on our King, and our life in his kingdom. If his Father had not been on his side, Jesus would still be in the grave. Those enemies who had sought so long to trap him, and then mocked him as he died a criminal's death—and the evil one, who stood behind them—would have been victorious. But God is on his King's side. **Read Philippians 2:6-11** with Psalm 124 in mind.

And if God were not on his people's side, we would have no hope. Sin would have a stranglehold, death would be a disaster and hell would be our destiny. Change would be a fantasy, confidence would be fleeting or groundless and joy would prove elusive. But God is on his people's side. **Read Romans 8:28-39** with Psalm 124 in mind.

Pray

Lord, if you were not on my side, it doesn't bear thinking about. Thank you that as you raised your Son from the dead, so you have raised me from spiritual death and will bring me to resurrection life. Thank you that you have sprung me from the trap of hell. Thank you that you are at work in and through me each day. Let me live in the joyful confidence that comes from knowing you are with me and for me. Amen.

CHRISTMAS: Who is Jesus?

As Christmas starts to feel very close, we are going to enjoy the first few chapters of Matthew's Gospel.

But we'll start with an overview of some of the facets of Jesus that Matthew focuses on.

Fulfilment of Scripture

Read Matthew 13:52

- *What do you think might be the "old treasures" that Jesus mentions?*
- *And what do you think are the "new"?*

Matthew goes out of his way to spotlight the links between the OT and Jesus. Seven times in the opening chapters, he says something like "This took place to fulfil what the Lord had said through the prophet" before citing a passage from the Old Testament (1:22; 2:5, 15, 17-18, 23; 3:3; 4:13-16).

Hope of the nations

It's widely thought that in the first instance Matthew wrote for Jewish believers or maybe Jewish seekers—yet despite this, Matthew is concerned throughout his Gospel to portray Jesus as the Saviour of all nations.

Read Acts 15:1-2

- *Why might Matthew be concerned to show his readers that Jesus is the Saviour of the Gentiles?*

Jesus fulfils both the promise to Abraham that God will bless all nations and the promise to Isaiah that a Servant will come in whose name the nations will put their hope (Matthew 1:1; 12:17-21).

God with us

Read Matthew 1:23

Mark and Luke let the evidence for the divinity of Jesus gradually build. But Matthew is explicit about this claim throughout his Gospel. When Jesus walks on water, for example, only Matthew describes the disciples declaring, "Truly you are the Son of God" (14:33).

Jesus is Immanuel, God with us. That was true during his life on the earth; and it continues to be true, for in the final words of Matthew's Gospel, Jesus says, "Surely I am with you always, to the very end of the age" (28:20).

Head of the church

Only Matthew describes the church as "the light of the world", a community whose distinctive life reveals God to the lost (5:14-16).

Read Matthew 18:1-10

Matthew portrays the embryonic church as a community of "little ones". We only enter the kingdom of heaven if we come like little children, and we're not to despise the lowly and least among us.

Pray

As we begin looking at Matthew and thinking about whose birth Christmas celebrates, pray that your eyes would be open to the wonder of all that Jesus is to you.

God's word fulfilled

Imagine turning on the TV at random to find you're watching the end of a crime drama. This is the key reveal—but you can't understand it because you've only just tuned in.

It's a bit like this if you first tune in to Jesus with the account of his birth. This is the key moment in the Bible story—but if you start at this point, you're going to struggle to understand what's going on. So Matthew packs his account of the Nativity with references to the Old Testament, to help us catch up with the story so far.

Read Matthew 1:1-17

- *Which key biblical figures does Matthew link Jesus to (v 1)?*
- *Why do you think this genealogy would be a good place to start for Matthew's Jewish readers?*
- *Which moments in the genealogy does Matthew give us more detail about?*
- *How does Matthew order his list (v 17)?*

Seven represents perfection or completion, and three fourteens are six sevens, so perhaps Matthew is wanting to portray Jesus as the seventh seven—the climax and pinnacle of God's purposes. What's clear is that Matthew's groups of fourteen focus on three key points:

1. Abraham: the father of the nation (v 2)
2. David: Israel's greatest king (v 6)
3. Babylon: the time when the Jews went into exile (v 12)

We're going to look at the first of these crucial moments in Bible history that led up to Jesus' birth.

From curse to blessing

Read Genesis 12:2-3

- *In what ways does God promise to make Abraham great (v 2)?*
- *How is it a promise to us too (v 3)?*

"Blessing" here doesn't simply mean "good things". When humanity rejected God, we became enemies of God, our relationships with one another became strained, and we were exiled from Eden (Genesis 3). Even the land was cursed, becoming prone to famine and disasters. But in Genesis 12 God promised that through Abraham's offspring, the curse would be reversed. Our relationship with God would be restored, human relationships would be mended, and the earth would be made new. This is the "blessing". The message of Matthew's genealogy is that this promise has passed down the generations... until we meet Mary and her child.

- *Read Galatians 3:13-14. How is Jesus going to bring this blessing?*

Pray

Give thanks that God's plan from the beginning was always to rescue us from our sin and suffering. Praise God for the fact of Jesus' birth over 2,000 years ago and for how his life, death, resurrection and ascension have transformed your future to be one full of blessing.

Home free

Today we look at some other key moments in the Bible's history which Matthew gives us as a foundation for understanding and appreciating the birth of Jesus.

From slavery to freedom

Read 2 Samuel 7:11b-16

After we rebelled against him, God had every reason to write us off. But instead he made a promise to David, Israel's greatest king, that one of his descendants would set God's people free—free to enjoy life under God's rule. There was a glimpse of this in the reigns of David and his son Solomon. But, by the time Matthew wrote, things had gone horribly wrong. Instead of restoring God's reign, successive kings led people further from God. But the prophets had promised a new King David, who would restore God's life-giving rule.

Apply

- *Who do you know who needs to understand the good news of freedom in Christ?*
- *How can you share this with them and pray for them today?*

From exile to home

Read Nehemiah 9:36-37

The history of ancient Israel ended in disaster: Exile in Babylon. The underlying issues of human sin and divine judgment had not been addressed. The Exile in Babylon was a picture of humanity's plight. We're all exiles from Eden, and we're all estranged from God. That's why we're so restless. Our hearts are hardwired for God, and yet it's as if we'll head in any direction except back to God, looking for fulfilment in our careers, homes, families or entertainment.

The message of Matthew's genealogy is that the end of exile is lying in the manger. Jesus is the one who will lead us home. He not only shows us the way back to God; he himself is "the way" (John 14:6).

A way home for all

Read Matthew 1:1-17

- *How does Matthew describe Jesus (v 1, 16)?*

Israelite kings were anointed with oil, so the promised king was known as "the anointed one"—the "Christ" (in Greek) or "Messiah" (in Hebrew). Jesus is God's promised King, coming to set not only Israel but humanity free.

- *Who are the four mothers interspersed in Matthew's genealogy (v 3, 5, 6)?*

Woven into a genealogy designed to establish Jesus' Jewish credentials are four Gentile women—a picture of the way Jesus will weave all nations into the story of God's people. These names break Matthew's pattern of "[was] the father of" to spotlight the fact that Jesus came to save Jews and Gentiles, men and women, sinners and sinned-against. It's a truth Matthew is about to reinforce as he explains the naming of Jesus.

Call him Immanuel

Matthew follows his genealogy with four stories surrounding the birth of Jesus, each of which contains a quote from the Old Testament. Let's revisit the familiar story.

Read Matthew 1:18-20

- *How does Mary conceive (v 18)?*

The word "birth" (v 18) is literally "genesis". The same word is used in v 1 ("genealogy" in the NIV), so the Gospel literally begins "[the] book of genesis". The Old Testament is about to be fulfilled and replayed. Just as the first Adam was given life through the Spirit (Genesis 2:7), so Jesus, the second Adam, is given human existence through the Spirit in the genesis of a new humanity.

- *In what way does Matthew present Joseph (Matthew 1:19)? What do we learn about his character?*
- *What does the angel tell Joseph (v 20), and how reassuring do you think this would have been for him?*

Two acts of naming

Read Matthew 1:21-25

- *What reason does the angel give for naming the baby as Jesus?*
- *For what reason will he be called Immanuel (v 23)?*

Matthew emphasises the fulfilment of the centuries' old promise by quoting from the book of Isaiah (v 23). This baby is going to deal with the problem of human sin and divine judgment—and it is God himself who is coming to save his people from sin. In his humanity Jesus is the descendant of David; in his divinity he is Immanuel, God with us.

TIME OUT

Read Isaiah 7:1-14

In Isaiah's day the house of David—the means through which God had promised to restore his reign—was in mortal danger. Isaiah promised divine deliverance if King Ahaz would entrust himself to God (v 3-9). God even offered to give Ahaz a sign (v 11). But Ahaz refused (v 12), opting instead for an alliance with Assyria (the rising superpower of the day).

- *Unlike how Ahaz acted, how should we respond to the promise of God even in the face of the difficulties life brings (Isaiah 7:4)?*

Apply

- *Spend some time thinking through how Immanuel, God with us, Jesus, our Saviour, brings us hope...*
  - *in a cursed world with broken relationships?*
  - *in a rebellious world in which people mock God and disregard his reign?*
  - *in a restless world in which people are exiled from God?*

Pray

In the struggles you're facing, pray: *My Jesus, Saviour, save me from sin and self today. My Immanuel, God with us, be with me today. Amen.*

Christmas gifts

HAPPY CHRISTMAS! It's time to meet the Magi (probably Persian astrologers), and to think about the significance of Matthew's second Old Testament quote.

Following yonder star

Matthew's Gospel is widely thought to have been written in the first place for Jewish readers. Yet Matthew is also interested in how salvation goes beyond Judaism to the world. This is exemplified in the story of the Magi.

Read Matthew 2:1-8

- *What is the Magi's purpose in travelling to Jerusalem (v 2)?*
- *What further knowledge do they need in order to find the Messiah (v 2)?*
- *Why do you think Herod and the Jerusalem elites are disturbed by what the Magi say (v 3)?*
- *What do you think is the reason for Herod's secrecy (v 7)?*

It's striking that those who know most about the Messiah welcome him least.

A child for all nations

Read Micah 3:9 – 4:5

- *How does the prophet Micah's tone change as he speaks about the people of Israel from the end of chapter 3 to the start of chapter 4?*
- *What is the hope given here for God's people (4:3-4)?*

From little Bethlehem will come a great king (Micah 5:2) who will shepherd God's people like David, Israel's original shepherd-king (5:4). This is Jesus, says Matthew (Matthew 2:5-6). Jesus will create a community which will attract and include people from all nations.

Bearing gifts

Read Matthew 2:9-12

The gifts of the Magi echo the story of the queen of Sheba bringing gifts to King Solomon (1 Kings 10:10) and Isaiah's promise of tribute from the nations (Isaiah 60:1-10; see also Psalm 72:10-11), including "gold and frankincense" (Isaiah 60:6, ESV).

- *What are the Magi's feelings and actions on finding Jesus (Matthew 2:10-11)?*
- *In contrast, what does verse 12 tell us about the true words and intentions of Herod in verse 8?*

Apply

Sadly, there's something of Herod in all of us. By nature we see Immanuel as a rival and are "disturbed" by the thought we might have to submit to his rule (v 3). Today, therefore, the challenge comes to us: are we going to see Jesus as a rival to eradicate from our lives or are we going to see Jesus as Immanuel and worship him with our lives?

- *How can you respond with both humility and joy at the coming of the Lord Jesus this Christmas Day?*

Bible in a year: Micah 4 – 5 • Luke 22:1-20

Out of Egypt

Christmas may be over, but the story of Jesus' family is not. Joseph must take Jesus to Egypt to escape the murderous intent of Herod, and so Jesus begins his life as a refugee.

Weeping and mourning

Read Matthew 2:13-18

- *What would the events of verse 14 have been like and felt like, do you think?*
- *What Old Testament Bible story does verse 16 bring to mind? (Hint: read Exodus 1.)*

Read Hosea 11:1-11

Hosea 11 begins by looking back to the way God led Israel out of Egypt through the Exodus (v 1-4). The odd thing is that when Matthew quotes from Hosea it is when Jesus escapes to Egypt (in Matthew 2:15) rather than when Jesus returns from Egypt (in v 21). This is because faithless Israel has become the latest manifestation of "Egypt", with a king massacring children just as Pharaoh once did (v 16; see Exodus 1). Once, Israel "my son" escaped from Egypt (Exodus 4:22-23); now, Jesus the Son escapes from "Egypt" into Egypt.

The nation of Israel has failed to live as a faithful son of God. But Jesus is a new Israel, the true person/people of God. Like Israel, Jesus comes out of Egypt. But unlike Israel, Jesus is a faithful son of God. God has not given up on his people; he's sent Jesus, the true Son, to be faithful on our behalf and to lead us home.

Apply

From the very beginning of his life, Jesus learnt what it is to be truly human, with all its uncertainties and dangers.

- *What difference does it make to your relationship with Jesus that he can sympathise with you in your weaknesses? (See Hebrews 4:15; 5:8-10.)*

Despised and rejected

Read Matthew 2:19-23

- *How does Joseph respond to the angel of the Lord's prompting (v 21)?*
- *In what kind of a town does it sound like Jesus grew up in (v 22-23)?*

There's no specific prophecy that speaks of the Messiah as a Nazarene, and Matthew's use of "prophets" (plural, v 23) suggests he's summing up a prophetic theme rather than referring to a specific text. It seems Matthew is using "Nazarene" as a derogatory slang term for someone coming from an insignificant place like Nazareth in Galilee.

Pray

If you serve in an out-of-the-way place or with marginal people, you may not make a name for yourself, but you are following in the steps of your Lord!

Praise the Lord that Jesus did not come to earth to live a privileged, wealthy, unrelatable life, but that he lowered himself to a humble life of hardship and insignificance for our sakes.

Bible in a year: Micah 6 – 7 • Luke 22:21-46

Jesus comes to...

Matthew introduces a new character in chapter 3: John the Baptist.

... liberate God's people

Read Matthew 3:1-6

- *What circumstances in the Isaiah quote (v 3) are reflected in the person of John the Baptist (v 1)?*
- *What does John's message imply is happening (v 2)?*

Matthew's quote from Isaiah 40:3 points to the significance of John's arrival. In chapter 40 of Isaiah, the prophet promises an end to exile through a new exodus. "Comfort, comfort my people," says God (v 1). Matthew's point is this: this comfort is on its way.

- *How do the people (and we) prepare for the coming of the Lord (Matthew 2:2)? And how is this expressed (v 6)?*

John's appearance (v 4) would have reminded Matthew's readers of the prophet Elijah, who was recognised by his hair coat and leather belt (2 Kings 1:8). Elijah was taken up to heaven without dying, so the expectation arose that he would return to announce the coming of the Lord (2 Kings 2:1, 11; Malachi 4:5).

... purge God's people

Read Matthew 3:7-9

- *How does John approach the Pharisees and Sadducees who have come to see what all the fuss is about (v 8)?*
- *What presumption of theirs does John tackle (v 9)?*

TIME OUT

Read Isaiah 10:24-25, 33-34

In this passage, God is about to cut down Assyria. In Matthew 3:10, that axe is poised over Israel. John imagines a lumberjack positioning his axe at the bottom of a tree trunk. But Isaiah continues: "A shoot will come up from the stump of Jesse; from his roots a Branch will bear fruit" (Isaiah 11:1).

God can create a new people, with a new king, out of judgment. Jesus is, as it were, going to cut out the trees who don't produce good fruit.

Apply

- *What does "fruit in keeping with repentance" look like in your own life?*
- *What "fruit" would you like to ask God to grow more in you, by his Spirit?*

Pray

What happened in first-century Israel is happening today throughout the world as the gospel is proclaimed. The message of Jesus divides humanity. And one day Jesus will return to enact judgment.

How can we prepare for this coming? We can confess our sins and "produce fruit in keeping with repentance" (Matthew 3:8). Come to him in repentance now, in the knowledge that Jesus has secured your forgiveness and new life in him.

Anointed and empowered

There's now a strange twist in Matthew's story. John says that Jesus is a greater person with a greater baptism than his. But then Jesus comes to be baptised by John!

Jesus baptises

Read Matthew 3:11-12

- *What is the contrast between John's baptism and Jesus' baptism (v 11)?*
- *What picture does John paint of Jesus (v 12)?*

We often contrast the outward cleansing of John's baptism with the inner cleansing of Jesus' work; Jesus cleanses our heart through the work of the Spirit. But Matthew's focus is on another type of cleansing or baptism: Jesus will judge unfruitful people just as farmers burn unfruitful trees or chaff (v 10, 12).

Jesus is baptised

Read Matthew 3:13-17

- *In the light of what he says in verses 11-12, why does John try to dissuade Jesus from being baptised (v 14)?*

John's baptism is a sign of repentance linked to the confession of sin (v 2, 6).

- *What question(s) does this raise about Jesus wanting John to baptise him?*

By being baptised, Jesus is obeying God's will and identifying with his sinful people. In doing so he accepts the role of the suffering servant to which God has called him. Jesus fulfils righteousness by signalling his willingness to obey God's will, which for him will mean suffering for his people. This resolution is affirmed as Jesus rises from the water. The "suffering servant" is first introduced in Isaiah 42:1 with these words: "Here is my servant, whom I uphold, my chosen one in whom I delight; I will put my Spirit on him, and he will bring justice to the nations". So it is that as Jesus rises from the water, the Spirit descends "on him", and the voice of the Father echoes Isaiah's word (Matthew 3:16-17).

Read Isaiah 42:1

- *What parallels do you notice between this prophecy and Matthew's account of God's words in Matthew 3:17?*

Pray

Water in the Bible story often represents judgment (Noah and the flood being the obvious example). This might be why Matthew highlights that Jesus "went up out of the water" (v 16). This baptism in water is a sign.

Spend some time thanking God for the real baptism Jesus endured when he was immersed in divine judgment on the cross for our sake (Mark 10:38). And that Jesus emerged from judgment in triumph.

Thank God that, if you are baptised into Christ, God declares over you: *You are my son, my daughter, whom I love; with you I am well pleased* (adapting Matthew 3:17).

- *What difference would remembering and believing that make to you today?*

Bible in a year: Zechariah 5 – 8 • Luke 23:1-25

Jesus passes the test

Do you like exams? Of course not. No one does. So much is at stake. Fail and you don't get a job or you're not allowed to drive or you can't go to university.

What if there were an exam to see if you could be part of God's people? In Matthew 4 just such an examination takes place! What's more, we all pass with flying colours—in and through Jesus.

Test #1

Read Matthew 4:1-4

At his baptism, Jesus fulfilled all righteousness by accepting the role of the suffering servant. To fulfil that role, Jesus laid down his privileges as God's Son (Philippians 2:6).

- *How is Satan's first temptation an invitation to take up those privileges again (Matthew 4:2-3)?*

Adam sinned by eating because he doubted God's word; Jesus obeyed by abstaining because God's word sustained him (v 4).

Test #2

Read Matthew 4:5-7

- *What is Satan trying to get Jesus to prove in this second test (v 5)?*

Later in Matthew's Gospel when Jesus is arrested, one of his companions draws his sword, but Jesus tells him to put it away: "Do you think I cannot call on my Father, and he will at once put at my disposal more than twelve legions of angels? But how then would the Scriptures be fulfilled that say it must happen in this way?" (26:53-54). The "angel option" is always there. But it would be opting out of the task God has given Jesus—the task of being the servant who suffers for his people.

Test #3

Read Matthew 4:8-11

- *All subtleties are dropped with Satan's third test. How does Jesus respond differently this time (v 10)?*

Apply

- *In what ways are you struggling with facing temptation currently?*
- *How does remembering that we are children of God and trusting in his fatherly care help us to resist temptaion?*
- *How can you extinguish the flaming arrows of Satan's temptations and lies by countering them with the promises of God's word? (See Ephesians 6:16.)*

First and foremost, we're to see ourselves not so much as "like Jesus" as "in Jesus". I'm not simply left trying harder to be like Christ. I can rest assured that I've already passed the test in Christ.

Pray

Praise your Father in heaven that he already sees you as an obedient child of his because Jesus has obeyed on your behalf.

Jesus lights up the world

When John the Baptist is imprisoned, Jesus withdraws to Galilee. Matthew suggests that Jesus went there to fulfil the prophecy of Isaiah 9:1-2.

A new dawn

Read Matthew 4:12-17

- *How do Jesus' actions show he hasn't gone to Galilee to try to avoid John's fate (v 17)?*
- *Why does Matthew say he went (v 14)?*

Centuries before, when the northern empire of Assyria had conquered Israel, the darkness of the Assyrian invasion had fallen first on the northern tribes of Zebulun and Naphtali (v 15). But Isaiah had promised that they would be the first to see the light when God came to liberate his people. Matthew says that that's now happening, through the ministry of Jesus. A new era is coming.

That day will fully arrive only at the end of history. But already the first rays of dawn have appeared over Galilee (v 16). Meanwhile the religious elites in Jerusalem remain in darkness.

A call to action

Read Matthew 4:18-22

- *What is distinctive about the way both Simon and Andrew and then James and John follow Jesus (v 20, 22)?*

Here we see a recurring characteristic of Matthew's: he pares stories down to their essential point. In Luke's account of this story, Simon Peter has had a frustrating night when Jesus tells him to try to catch fish once more. The result is a miraculous haul of fish, and Peter has to call for help. Matthew ignores all this and instead zones in on the key thing for his readers (including us): "Come, follow me ... and I will send you out to fish for people" (Matthew 4:19).

Apply

Take time to ask yourself these questions:

- *What is it that Jesus is asking me to leave behind?*
- *How can I seek to "fish for people"?*

A glimpse ahead

Read Matthew 4:23-25

Verse 23 is repeated in 9:35 to create two bookends to Matthew 5 – 9. This particular section is a kind of preview: we're going to see Jesus proclaiming good news in chapters 5 – 7 and demonstrating that good news in miraculous healings in chapters 8 – 9.

Pray

The life of Jesus offers a glimpse of God's coming new world.

- *How does reflecting on this truth excite and/or comfort you?*

Pray that, as you spend time reflecting on the life of Jesus in Matthew, you will experience the comfort of God and that your faith would be revitalised.

Bible in a year: Zechariah 13 – 14 • Luke 24:1-35

Happy are those...

We end the year with the first part of the Sermon on the Mount and Jesus' famous Beatitudes. These are great words to have ringing in our ears as we move into 2027...

Liberation for the nation

Matthew 1 – 4 presents Jesus as the liberator who will end the exile through a new exodus and lead God's people home. The longed-for liberation is happening—though not in the way most Jews have been expecting. This theme of liberation continues in the Beatitudes...

Read Matthew 5:1-12

- *Are there any verses that the Jews who were listening to Jesus might have interpreted as being about freedom from the Roman rule that they hoped for, do you think?*
- *Which verses may have confused them?*

Jesus is speaking of something much bigger than political liberation. He has come to liberate his people from sin and death—to end the curse of Genesis 3 and establish a kingdom of blessing. Matthew 5:4-9 all point to the future ("they will..."). In the meantime, the followers of Jesus are not to be violent revolutionaries but "peacemakers" (v 9).

Invitation to the broken

"Blessed" can be a bit of a misleading translation because it implies something that is done and dusted. The Beatitudes are not entrance requirements of Christ's kingdom, nor rewards for good behaviour. They're descriptions of how we can live a blessed life under Christ's kingship. The second half of each Beatitude then explains why this is the best way to live even when this life is accompanied by sorrow, suffering and brokenness.

- *What's different about the blessing in verses 11-12? Who is Jesus addressing here and why does this persecution come?*

Pray

Spend a moment in prayer for Christians you know or Christians in other areas of the world who are particularly suffering as a result of their faith in Jesus. Pray that they would know blessing and joy.

Apply

To end today's study, let's do an exercise in opposites and imagine the reverse of each statement Jesus makes. It might go something like this: *Believe in yourself because you're great as you are!* (The opposite of verse 3.) *Don't take life too seriously and shrug it off when you make mistakes* (v 4). *Always look after No. 1 and don't let anyone put you down* (v 5).

- *Spend some time imagining the opposites of the rest of the verses. Which are you tempted to believe?*
- *Which one true Beatitude do you most want to shape your perspective next year?*

We will pick up in Matthew again after a set of New Year studies.